YOUR PERSONAL

ASTROLOGY

GUIDE

AQUARIUS
2013

YOUR PERSONAL
ASTROLOGY
GUIDE

AQUARIUS
2013

RICK LEVINE **& JEFF** JAWER

STERLING ETHOS
New York

STERLING ETHOS
New York

An Imprint of Sterling Publishing
387 Park Avenue South
New York, NY 10016

ISBN 978-1-4027-7954-1

Distributed in Canada by Sterling Publishing
c/o Canadian Manda Group, 165 Dufferin Street
Toronto, Ontario, Canada M6K 3H6
Distributed in the United Kingdom by GMC Distribution Services
Castle Place, 166 High Street, Lewes, East Sussex, England BN7 1XU
Distributed in Australia by Capricorn Link (Australia) Pty. Ltd.
P.O. Box 704, Windsor, NSW 2756, Australia

For information about custom editions, special sales, and premium
and corporate purchases, please contact Sterling Special Sales at
800-805-5489 or specialsales@sterlingpublishing.com.

Manufactured in the United States of America

2 4 6 8 10 9 7 5 3 1

www.sterlingpublishing.com

TABLE OF CONTENTS

Author's Note:

Your Personal Astrology Guide uses the Tropical zodiac based on the seasons, not the constellations. This method of determining signs has been and continues to be the practice of Western astrologers for over 2,000 years. Aries, the beginning of the Tropical zodiac, starts on the first day of spring every year. Contrary to what you may have heard, no one's sign has changed, regardless of when you were born and the addition of a thirteenth sign is not relevant to Western astrology.

Measuring and recording the apparent movement of the Sun, the Moon, and the planets against the backdrop of the heavens is a complex task because nothing is stationary. Even the location of the constellations with respect to the seasons gradually changes from year to year. Since astrologers are concerned with human behavior here on Earth, they created a twelve-fold zodiac that is anchored to four seasons as their primary frame of reference. Obviously, astrologers fully understand that there are eighty-eight official constellations and that the moving planets travel through many of them (including Ophiuchus and Orion), but these are not—and never have been—part of the Tropical zodiac created by astrologers.

THE PURPOSE OF THIS BOOK

The more you learn about yourself, the better able you are to wisely use the energies in your life.
For more than 3,000 years, astrology has been the sharpest tool in the box for describing the human condition. Used by virtually every culture on the planet, astrology continues to serve as a link between individual lives and planetary cycles. We gain valuable insights into personal issues with a birth chart, and can plot the patterns of the year ahead in meaningful ways for individuals as well as groups. You share your sun sign with eight percent of humanity. Clearly, you're not all going to have the same day, even if the basic astrological cycles are the same. Your individual circumstances, the specific factors of your entire birth chart, and your own free will help you write your unique story.

The purpose of this book is to describe the energies of the Sun, Moon, and planets for the year ahead and help you create your future, rather than being a victim of it. We aim to facilitate your journey by showing you the turns ahead in the road of life and hopefully the best ways to navigate them.

YOU ARE THE STAR OF YOUR LIFE

It is not our goal to simply predict events. Rather, we are reporting the planetary energies—the cosmic weather in which you are living—so that you understand these conditions and know how to use them most effectively.

The power, though, isn't in the stars, but in your mind, your heart, and the choices that you make every day. Regardless of how strongly you are buffeted by the winds of change or bored by stagnation, you have many ways to view any situation. Learning about the energies of the Sun, Moon, and planets will both sharpen and widen your perspective, thereby giving you additional choices.

The language of astrology is a gift of awareness, not a rigid set of rules. It works best when blended with common sense, intuition, and self-trust. This is your life, and no one knows how to live it as well as you. Take what you need from this book and leave the rest. Although the planets set the stage for the year ahead, you're the writer, director, and star of your life and you can play the part in whatever way you choose. *Your Personal Astrology Guide* uses information about your sun sign to give you a better understanding of how the planetary waves will wash upon your shore. We each navigate our lives through time, and each moment has unique qualities. Astrology gives us the ability to describe the constantly changing timescape. For example, if you know the trajectory and the speed of an approaching storm, you can choose to delay a leisurely afternoon sail on the bay, thus avoiding an unpleasant situation.

By reading this book, you can improve your ability to align with the cosmic weather, the larger patterns that affect you day to day. You can become more effective by aligning with the cosmos and cocreating the year ahead with a better understanding of the energies around you.

Astrology doesn't provide quick fixes to life's complex issues. It doesn't offer neatly packed black-and-white answers in a world filled with an infinite variety of shapes and colors. It can, however, give you a much clearer picture of the invisible forces influencing your life.

ENERGY & EVENTS

Two sailboats can face the same gale yet travel in opposite directions as a result of how the sails are positioned. Similarly, how you respond to the energy of a particular set of circumstances may be more responsible for your fate than the given situation itself. We delineate the energetic winds for your year ahead, but your attitude shapes the unfolding events, and your responses alter your destiny.

This book emphasizes the positive, not because all is good, but because astrology shows us ways to transform even the power of a storm into beneficial results. Empowerment comes from learning to see the invisible energy patterns that impact the visible landscape as you fill in the details of your story every day on this spinning planet, orbited by the Moon, lit by the Sun, and colored by the nuances of the planets.

You are a unique point in an infinite galaxy of unlimited possibilities, and the choices that you make have consequences. So use this book in a most magical way to consciously improve your life.

MOON CHARTS

2013 NEW MOONS

Each New Moon marks the beginning of a cycle. In general, this is the best time to plant seeds for future growth. Use the days preceeding the New Moon to finish old business prior to starting what comes next. The focused mind can be quite sharp during this phase. Harness the potential of the New Moon by stating your intentions—out loud or in writing—for the weeks ahead. Hold these goals in your mind and help them grow to fruition through conscious actions as the Moon gains light during the following two weeks. In the chart below, the dates and times refer to when the Moon and Sun align in each zodiac sign (see p. 16), initiating a new lunar cycle.

DATE	TIME	SIGN
January 11	2:43 pm EST	Capricorn
February 10	2:20 am EST	Aquarius
March 11	3:51 pm EDT	Pisces
April 10	5:35 am EDT	Aries
May 9	8:28 pm EDT	Taurus (ECLIPSE)
June 8	11:56 am EDT	Gemini
July 8	3:14 am EDT	Cancer
August 6	5:50 pm EDT	Leo
September 5	7:36 am EDT	Virgo
October 4	8:34 pm EDT	Libra
November 3	7:49 am EST	Scorpio (ECLIPSE)
December 2	7:22 pm EST	Sagittarius

2013 FULL MOONS

The Full Moon reflects the light of the Sun as subjective feelings reflect the objective events of the day. Dreams seem bigger; moods feel stronger. The emotional waters run with deeper currents. This is the phase of culmination, a turning point in the energetic cycle. Now it's time to listen to the inner voices. Rather than starting new projects, the two weeks after the Full Moon are when we complete what we can and slow our outward expressions in anticipation of the next New Moon. In this chart, the dates and times refer to when the moon is opposite the sun in each zodiac sign, marking the emotional peak of each lunar cycle.

DATE	TIME	SIGN
January 26	11:38 pm EST	Leo
February 25	3:26 pm EST	Virgo
March 27	5:27 am EDT	Libra
April 25	3:57 pm EDT	Scorpio (ECLIPSE)
May 25	12:24 am EDT	Sagittarius
June 23	7:32 am EDT	Capricorn
July 22	2:15 pm EDT	Aquarius
August 20	9:44 pm EDT	Aquarius
September 19	7:12 am EDT	Pisces
October 18	7:37 pm EDT	Aries (ECLIPSE)
November 17	10:15 am EST	Taurus
December 17	4:28 am EST	Gemini

ASTROLOGY, YOU & THE WORLD

WELCOME TO YOUR SUN SIGN

The Sun, Moon, and Earth and all the planets lie within a plane called the **ecliptic** and move through a narrow band of stars made up by 12 constellations called the **zodiac**. The Earth revolves around the Sun once a year, but from our point of view, it appears that the Sun moves through each sign of the zodiac for one month. There are 12 months and astrologically there are 12 signs. The astrological months, however, do not match our calendar, and start between the 19th and 23rd of each month. Everyone is born to an astrological month, like being born in a room with a particular perspective of the world. Knowing your sun sign provides useful information about your personality and your future, but for a more detailed astrological analysis, a full birth chart calculation based on your precise date, time, and place of birth is necessary. Get your complete birth chart online at:

http://www.tarot.com/astrology/astroprofile

This book is about your zodiac sign. Your Sun is in the intellectual Aquarius, an objective air sign in spite of its watery name. The Water Bearer, your symbol, represents the mind of humanity elevating you above the instincts of your emotions. You're idealistic and friendly, but often in a cool, detached way, since you typically need space to express your individuality and don't like clingy people. You're a visionary for the future who usually doesn't like to look back.

THE PLANETS

We refer to the Sun and Moon as planets. Don't worry; we do know about modern astronomy. Although the Sun is really a star and the Moon is a satellite, they are called planets for astrological purposes. The astrological planets are the Sun, the Moon, Mercury, Venus, Mars, Jupiter, Saturn, Chiron, Uranus, Neptune, and Pluto.

Your sun sign is the most obvious astrological placement, for the Sun returns to the same sign every year. But at the same time, the Moon is orbiting the Earth, changing signs every two and a third days. Mercury, Venus, and Mars each move through a sign in a few weeks to a few months. Jupiter spends a whole year in a sign—and Pluto visits a sign for up to 30 years! The ever-changing positions of the planets alter the energetic terrain through which we travel. The planets are symbols; each has a particular range of meanings. For example, Venus is the goddess of love, but it really symbolizes beauty in a spectrum of experiences. Venus can represent romantic love, sensuality, the arts, or good food. It activates anything that we value, including personal possessions and even money. To our ancestors, the planets actually animated life on Earth. In this way of thinking, every beautiful flower contains the essence of Venus.

Each sign has a natural affinity to an individual planet, and as this planet moves through the sky, it sends messages of particular interest to people born under that sign. Saturn, your traditional key or ruling planet, represents the scientific and rational part of your personality and shows where you encounter hard, cold reality. Your sign's modern ruler, Uranus, triggers brilliant ideas and provokes original behavior that sets you apart from the pack. Planets can be described by many different words, for the mythology of each is a rich tapestry. In this book we use a variety of words when talking about each planet in order to convey the most applicable meaning. The table below describes a few keywords for each planet, including the Sun and Moon.

PLANET	SYMBOL	KEYWORDS
Sun	☉	Consciousness, Will, Vitality
Moon	☽	Subconscious, Emotions, Habits
Mercury	☿	Communication, Thoughts, Transportation
Venus	♀	Desire, Love, Money, Values
Mars	♂	Action, Physical Energy, Drive
Jupiter	♃	Expansion, Growth, Optimism
Saturn	♄	Contraction, Maturity, Responsibility
Chiron	⚷	Healing, Pain, Subversion
Uranus	♅	Awakening, Unpredictable, Inventive
Neptune	♆	Imagination, Spirituality, Confusion
Pluto	♇	Passion, Intensity, Regeneration

HOUSES

Just as planets move through the signs of the zodiac, they also move through the houses in an individual chart. The 12 houses correspond to the 12 signs, but are individualized, based upon your sign. In this book we use Solar Houses, which place your sun sign in your 1st House. Therefore, when a planet enters a new sign it also enters a new house. If you know your exact time of birth, the rising sign determines the 1st House. You can learn your rising sign by entering your birth date at:

http://www.tarot.com/astrology/astroprofile

HOUSE	SIGN	KEYWORDS
1st House	Aries	Self, Appearance, Personality
2nd House	Taurus	Possessions, Values, Self-Worth
3rd House	Gemini	Communication, Siblings, Short Trips
4th House	Cancer	Home, Family, Roots
5th House	Leo	Love, Romance, Children, Play
6th House	Virgo	Work, Health, Daily Routines
7th House	Libra	Marriage, Relationships, Business Partners
8th House	Scorpio	Intimacy, Transformation, Shared Resources
9th House	Sagittarius	Travel, Higher Education, Philosophy
10th House	Capricorn	Career, Community, Ambition
11th House	Aquarius	Groups and Friends, Associations, Social Ideals
12th House	Pisces	Imagination, Spirituality, Secret Activities

ASPECTS

As the planets move through the sky in their various cycles, they form ever-changing angles with one another. Certain angles create significant geometric shapes. So, when two planets are 90 degrees apart, they conform to a square; 60 degrees of separation conforms to a sextile, or six-pointed star. Planets create **aspects** when they're at these special angles. Aspects explain how the individual symbolism of pairs of planets combine into an energetic pattern.

ASPECT	DEGREES	KEYWORD
Conjunction	0	Compression, Blending, Focus
Opposition	180	Tension, Awareness, Balance
Trine	120	Harmony, Free-Flowing, Ease
Square	90	Resistance, Stress, Dynamic Conflict
Quintile	72	Creativity, Metaphysical, Magic
Sextile	60	Support, Intelligent, Activating
Quincunx	150	Irritation, Annoyance, Adjustment

2013 GENERAL FORECAST

Astrology works for individuals, groups, and humanity as a whole. You will have your own story in 2013, but it will unfold along with seven billion other tales of human experience. We are each unique, yet our lives touch one another; our destinies are woven together by weather and war, by the economy, science, music, politics, religion, and all the other threads of life on planet Earth.

This astrological look at the major trends and planetary patterns for 2013 provides a framework for comprehending the potentials and challenges we face together, so that we can move forward with tolerance and respect as a community as we also fulfill our potential as individuals.

The astrological events used for this forecast are the transits of major planets Jupiter and Saturn, the retrograde cycles of Mercury, and the eclipses of the Sun and the Moon.

A NOTE ABOUT DATES IN THIS BOOK

All events are based upon the Eastern Time Zone of the United States. Because of local time differences, an event occurring just a few minutes after midnight in the East will actually happen the prior day in the rest of the country. Although the key dates are the exact dates of any particular alignment, some of you are so ready for certain things to happen that you can react to a transit a day or two before it is exact. And sometimes you can be so entrenched in habits or unwilling to change that you may not notice the effects right away. Allow extra time around each key date to feel the impact of any event.

JUPITER IN GEMINI:
LARGER THAN LIFE
June 11, 2012–June 25, 2013

Astrological tradition considers multifaceted Gemini an awkward place for truth-seeking Jupiter. We can be inundated with so much information that it's nearly impossible to see the forest for the trees. Jupiter's long-range vision may be obscured by a million and one ideas that scatter attention, diffusing the focus we need to achieve long-term goals. Yes, this mind-opening transit stirs curiosity about a wide variety of subjects—but it may be difficult to concentrate and gain in-depth knowledge in any one area if we're skimming the surface. Expansive Jupiter in communicative Gemini can also be quite verbose, valuing the volume of information more than its substance. Philosophical flexibility and mental versatility are gifts of this transit, while its less desirable qualities include inconsistency of beliefs and careless planning.

JUPITER IN CANCER:
FEELING IS BELIEVING
June 25, 2013–July 16, 2014

Philosophical Jupiter provides understanding through emotions during its stay in sensitive Cancer. We're likely to reject ideas that do not correspond to gut instincts, applying a subjective check against concepts that sound good but just don't feel right. Returning to traditional sources of wisdom and reconnecting with nature and family deepens our roots in the past to provide a needed sense of stability in these tumultuous times. Yet looking back for answers to today's questions has its limitations; conditions are changing so rapidly now that old rules no longer apply. We gain a sense of safety by relying on time-tested principles, but we may lose the potential for envisioning a creative new tomorrow by following these well-worn paths. The sentimental nature of Jupiter in Cancer favors familiar circles to unfamiliar. Given this transit's protective qualities, this makes it easier to justify closing the door to new people and experiences. Racism, nationalism, and religious and ethnic prejudices are more prevalent when mental gates close to outsiders. Yet Jupiter in nurturing Cancer, at its highest potential, helps us recognize the living nature of truth in an ever-growing spiral that draws upon the best of the old to nourish new goals and aspirations.

SATURN IN SCORPIO:
SHADOWBOXING
October 5, 2012–December 23, 2014
June 14, 2015–September 16, 2015

Responsible Saturn in formidable Scorpio tests our resolve. We are challenged to look into the dark corners of our psyches where fears about love, money, and mortality hide. It's tempting to turn away from these complicated subjects, yet the price of doing so is high because we are then controlled by unconscious impulses. Saturn in Scorpio reminds us that no one is entirely pure and simple. The complexities of giving and receiving affection, dealing with hidden desires, and working with manipulative people are numerous. But if we're willing to show up and do the work, Saturn also offers clarity and authority, enabling us to address these complicated matters. Taking responsibility for dark feelings doesn't mean that we must suppress them; it's a signal to engage them with patience rather than punishment. Personal and professional alliances work more effectively when we stop keeping secrets from ourselves. Finally, with Saturn in Scorpio we could see even more consolidation of financial institutions as a result of bad loans.

MERCURY RETROGRADES
February 23–March 17 in Pisces / June 26–July 20 in Cancer / October 21–November 10 in Scorpio

All true planets appear to move backward from time to time, because we view them from the moving platform of Earth. The most noticeable and regular retrograde periods are those of

Mercury, the communication planet. Occurring three or four times a year for roughly three weeks at a time, these are periods when difficulties with details, travel, communication, and technical matters are more common than usual.

Mercury's retrograde is often perceived as negative, but you can make this cycle work for you. Because personal and commercial interactions are emphasized, you can actually accomplish more than usual, especially if you stay focused on what you need to complete instead of initiating new projects. Still, you may feel as if you're treading water—or worse, being carried backward in an undertow of unfinished business. Worry less about making progress than about the quality of your work. Pay extra attention to all your communication exchanges. Avoiding misunderstandings and omissions is the ideal way to minimize complications. Retrograde Mercury is best used to tie up loose ends as you review, redo, reconsider, and, in general, revisit the past.

All three Mercury retrograde cycles occur in emotional water signs this year. This can make communication more difficult, because it's not easy to translate feelings into words. Our potential loss of objectivity, as well, can lead to even more misunderstandings than usual. Thankfully, these three periods give us the chance to reconnect with our emotions, which can inspire new waves of creativity.

ECLIPSES
Solar: May 9 and November 3
Lunar: April 25, May 25, and October 18

Solar and Lunar Eclipses are special New and Full Moons that indicate significant changes for individuals and groups. They are powerful markers of events, with influences that can appear up to three months in advance and last up to six months afterward.

April 25, Lunar Eclipse in Scorpio: Sink or Swim
This Lunar Eclipse in passionate Scorpio tells us to let go of the past and start living in the present. Taskmaster Saturn's conjunction to the Moon, though, encourages a tenacious attitude that can keep us entangled in unrewarding relationships. Resentment, jealousy, and revenge aren't worth the effort they take to sustain. However, initiating

Mars is conjunct to the sensible Taurus Sun, which favors simplifying life and making a fresh start instead of trying to fix an unresolvable problem.

May 9, Solar Eclipse in Taurus: Trim the Fat
The cost of comfort may become so high that we have to let go of laziness or of some luxuries to make life more affordable. There's a self-indulgent side to Taurus, and with combative Mars and talkative Mercury joined with the Sun and Moon, we can find ourselves aggressively defending our behavior. Yet trying to justify standing still and holding on to what we have may only increase the steep price we pay later for resisting the purging we need now.

May 25, Lunar Eclipse in Sagittarius: Life's an Adventure
An eclipse in farsighted Sagittarius reminds us to bring our attention back from some distant vision to focus on the here and now. We can discover alternative ways to make life work instead of acting as if there's only one road to fulfillment. Beliefs may not hold up in the face of changing

circumstances that require flexibility instead of certainty. Asking questions reveals options that multiply choices, creating confusion for some but freeing most of us from rigid thinking and excessive judgment.

October 18, Lunar Eclipse in Aries:
No Man Is an Island
Life is not a solo voyage even when we're feeling all alone. This eclipse emphasizes the need to work with others and demands some degree of compromise and accommodation. It's better to sit on the fence, gather more information, and mull things over than to race ahead impulsively now. While it may seem that sharing feelings with others hinders progress, it garners us support that overcomes the isolation of not accepting advice and assistance.

November 3, Solar Eclipse in Scorpio: Baby Steps
Expect power struggles controlling Saturn's conjunction to this New Moon Eclipse. It's not easy to trust people—and sometimes it's just as difficult to trust ourselves. This eclipse, however, is about backing away from pressure, reducing

intensity, and seeking peaceful moments in our lives. Recognizing the gifts that we're given every day can alleviate a profound feeling of hunger, perhaps even despair, through small moments of joy and pleasure.

THE BOTTOM LINE:
YELL FIRE!

The Mayan calendar may have turned over near the end of 2012, but the human story on this planet is far from complete. Nevertheless, we are still in the midst of a period of powerful change that began with the opposition of structural Saturn and explosive Uranus in late 2008, when we experienced the first wave of the worst financial crisis since the Great Depression, along with the subsequent election of Barack Obama. The year 2012 brought the first of seven tense squares between Uranus and transformational Pluto that will recur through 2015, shaking the very foundations of societies around the world. The volatile Uranus-Pluto square is exact on May 20 and November 1, April 21 and December 15, 2014, and March 16, 2015. The long-lasting connection between revolutionary Uranus and volcanic Pluto is already fomenting change on a grand scale, and this will continue for years to come.

It is tempting, though, to gaze back and seek to re-create the relative safety of the past. Joyful Jupiter's entry into cautious and conservative Cancer will bring waves of nostalgia for the "good old days," along with protectionist calls for stronger national borders. Yet the idea that we can return to the past is not a feasible one. The technological cats are out of the bag, and addressing environmental issues alone requires forward, not backward, thinking. Our challenge is to construct new realities based on bold visions and idealistic dreams of a world that does not yet exist. This takes courage in the face of confusion and confidence in the midst of chaos. It's tempting to call out to higher powers to rescue us from the consequences of our actions: suffering evokes cries for help. And yet we are capable of healing ourselves if we finally embrace the twenty-first century instead of retreating to mythical moments of an idealized past.

Inventive Uranus in pioneering Aries is opening new neural pathways that are reshaping our view of reality. Yes, we may encounter moments when thoughts are so strange that we may fear ourselves to be mad. But curious minds, flexible egos, and adaptable emotions allow us to glimpse a more enlightened, evolved, and competent humanity without breaking down. We are challenged to dance with the stranger who enters our heads with perceptions that don't readily fit into our existing intellectual framework. We must find new ways out of the dilemmas that we've created for ourselves. Embracing small discoveries and appreciating surprises are good training techniques: they prepare us to step up to the next level of human evolution and continue the remarkable journey of love and light on planet Earth.

Remember that all of these astrological events are part of the general cosmic weather of the year, but will affect us each differently based upon our individual astrological signs.

AQUARIUS
AUGUST–DECEMBER
2012 OVERVIEW

DO WHAT YOU LOVE, LOVE WHAT YOU DO

The month gets off to an auspicious start. A deliciously playful Full Moon in quirky Aquarius on **August 1** ignites an explosion of joy as bountiful Jupiter trines the Moon from your 5th House of Romance. If you've been feeling at odds in your personal and professional relationships, you should find your footing when communicative Mercury turns forward in your 7th House of Others on **August 8**. The audacious Leo New Moon on the **17th** brings another wave of self-confidence, goodwill, and supportive friends and co-workers. The extravagant ideas of your allies and the boldness of your own proposals gain credibility from a smart sextile to solid Saturn that provides the common sense and follow-through to turn your plans into reality.

Connecting with reliable people can strengthen the practical foundations on which your partnerships are built when the Sun enters loyal Virgo and your 8th House of Shared Resources on **August 22**. However, you could also feel nitpicked by petty thinkers or nagged by a worried lover or business associate. Rather than ignoring their concerns and complicating the situation by acting defensively, it's wiser to dig in and do the hard work of maintaining trust and developing more efficient teamwork. Active Mars's shift into intense Scorpio and your 10th House of Career on the **23rd** also calls you down from the clouds to concentrate your efforts where they're most needed. Financial uncertainties may come to light when the vulnerable Pisces Full Moon illuminates your 2nd House of Resources on **August 31**. Fortunately, a supportive sextile from perceptive Pluto shows you how to turn losses into gains and revive a creative interest for profit and pleasure.

WEDNESDAY 1 ★ ○ **SUPER NOVA DAYS** The spotlight is on you

THURSDAY 2 ★

FRIDAY 3

SATURDAY 4

SUNDAY 5

MONDAY 6

TUESDAY 7

WEDNESDAY 8

THURSDAY 9 ★ Bring an extra dose of creativity and commitment to your job

FRIDAY 10

SATURDAY 11

SUNDAY 12

MONDAY 13

TUESDAY 14

WEDNESDAY 15 ★ There's no room for nonsense now

THURSDAY 16 ★

FRIDAY 17 ★ ●

SATURDAY 18 ★

SUNDAY 19

MONDAY 20 ★ Finding the right pace may be difficult

TUESDAY 21 ★

WEDNESDAY 22 ★

THURSDAY 23

FRIDAY 24

SATURDAY 25

SUNDAY 26

MONDAY 27

TUESDAY 28 ★ Your ideas might be too far ahead of their time

WEDNESDAY 29

THURSDAY 30

FRIDAY 31 ○

★ designates key date

COMPLICATED CONNECTIONS

The complexities of relationships are key issues for much of the month with the analytical Virgo Sun in your 8th House of Deep Sharing until the Autumn Equinox on **September 22**. You may feel crowded in partnerships that infringe on your freedom. You face hard work to untangle misunderstandings and create more harmonious relationships. Don't despair if situations seem irresolvable; the Sun's entry into objective Libra on the **22nd** illuminates your 9th House of Higher Principles, broadening perspectives and enabling compromises. Thankfully, enticing Venus enters generous Leo and your 7th House of Others on **September 6**, which should attract enthusiastic allies. Enjoying the attention and encouragement of your peers can be exhilarating, yet promises may exceed performance, so restrain your expectations until someone has truly earned your trust.

The precise Virgo New Moon in your 8th House on the **15th** plants seeds of partnership possibilities—but if you want them to grow, you must be clear about your goals and willing to plan meticulously. The second explosive Uranus-Pluto square occurs on the **19th**—the first was on **June 24**—to help you give voice to your unexpressed desires. The thoughts and feelings exposed now raise complex questions that you might not resolve until the final Uranus-Pluto square on **March 16, 2015**. The tectonic shifts promised by this pair might also initiate crises during the Full Moon in Aries on **September 29** as you struggle to maintain your independence without shattering relationships. Striking Uranus's conjunction and stunning Pluto's square to the impulsive Aries Full Moon incite sharp words but can also thrill you with radical new ideas.

SATURDAY 1

SUNDAY 2

MONDAY 3

TUESDAY 4

WEDNESDAY 5

THURSDAY 6 ★ Watch out for a tendency to overindulge

FRIDAY 7 ★

SATURDAY 8

SUNDAY 9

MONDAY 10

TUESDAY 11

WEDNESDAY 12

THURSDAY 13 ★ A light touch helps you to work around resistance

FRIDAY 14

SATURDAY 15　　●

SUNDAY 16

MONDAY 17

TUESDAY 18

WEDNESDAY 19

THURSDAY 20 ★ Supercharged conversations put everyone on edge

FRIDAY 21

SATURDAY 22

SUNDAY 23

MONDAY 24 ★ **SUPER NOVA DAYS** You're reluctant to follow the rules

TUESDAY 25 ★

WEDNESDAY 26

THURSDAY 27

FRIDAY 28

SATURDAY 29 ★ ○ Make a quick getaway before anyone notices you're gone

SUNDAY 30

BALANCING ACT

This month is all about the relationship between your ideals and the execution of your strategy. October starts with the Sun in your 9th House of Big Ideas and finishes with it shining in your 10th House of Public Responsibility. The entry of agreeable Venus into pragmatic Virgo and your 8th House of Shared Resources on **October 3** puts a priority on efficiency, yet dashing Mars's move into theoretical Sagittarius and your 11th House of Community on the **6th** tends to value adherence to a cause above practicality. A similar contradiction is illustrated on **October 5** when mental Mercury joins dependable Saturn in the last degree of Libra in your 9th House before both planets move into Scorpio in your 10th House later that day. You may be able to articulate a perfect plan for bringing peace and justice into your life but then encounter limits imposed by your duties.

Fortunately, you can span the gap between hope and reality thanks to a creative trine between earthbound Saturn and heavenly Neptune on **October 10**. This favorable alignment, which recurs on **June 11** and **July 13, 2013**, widens your picture of reality until you find room for these seemingly opposing perspectives. You may not resolve the differences immediately, but you should begin to envision a future in which they can work together. On the **15th**, the diplomatic instincts that the Libra New Moon gives you are enriched with a trine to promising Jupiter. The Sun's entry into scrutinizing Scorpio on **October 22** and the Taurus Full Moon in your 4th House of Home and Family on the **29th** reveal the gulf between your personal and professional lives. The Sun's conjunction with strict Saturn on the **25th** requires you to set clear priorities, maintain focus, and develop patience.

MONDAY 1	
TUESDAY 2	
WEDNESDAY 3	
THURSDAY 4	
FRIDAY 5 ★	Mastery of information is critical
SATURDAY 6 ★	
SUNDAY 7 ★	
MONDAY 8	
TUESDAY 9 ★	**SUPER NOVA DAYS** Look beyond short-term issues
WEDNESDAY 10 ★	
THURSDAY 11	
FRIDAY 12	
SATURDAY 13	
SUNDAY 14	
MONDAY 15 ★ ●	Consolidate gains before you push ahead
TUESDAY 16	
WEDNESDAY 17	
THURSDAY 18	
FRIDAY 19	
SATURDAY 20 ★	Step back and try a simpler approach
SUNDAY 21 ★	
MONDAY 22	
TUESDAY 23	
WEDNESDAY 24	
THURSDAY 25	
FRIDAY 26	
SATURDAY 27	
SUNDAY 28 ★	Stay calm and narrow your focus
MONDAY 29 ★ ○	
TUESDAY 30	
WEDNESDAY 31	

LISTEN TO YOUR HEART

Your mind may be wrapped around professional issues for much of this month, but it's really your heart that could win out in the end. The emotionally powerful Scorpio Sun in your 10th House of Career stresses you out at work until **November 21**. Managing those below you or dealing with control from those above provokes you to look more deeply at your current position. The Scorpio New Moon on the **13th** is a Solar Eclipse that reminds you to invest more of yourself where you are— or look elsewhere for fulfillment on the job. You can't continue to drive yourself ahead on sheer will unless your inner commitment matches your external obligations. The dominance of intellect may also recede when cerebral Mercury is retrograde on **November 6–26**. The communication planet begins this period of reevaluation in your team-oriented 11th House and ends it in your individually responsible 10th House, which could reveal those areas where a lack of support from colleagues increases the burden on you.

You enjoy some much-needed relief from professional pressures when delightful Venus in Libra creates a sweet trine with indulgent Jupiter in Gemini on **November 9**. This harmonious connection between two social planets can brighten relationships and inspire romance. While you're likely to have a good time—even if reality falls short of your expectations—a joyous vision can also lift your spirits. On **November 28**, the Gemini Full Moon Lunar Eclipse in your 5th House of Love challenges you to stop playing around the edges of desire and finally make a choice that should be worth much more than you have to give up in return.

THURSDAY 1 ★ An unexpected event shakes up your life

FRIDAY 2 ★

SATURDAY 3 ★

SUNDAY 4

MONDAY 5

TUESDAY 6

WEDNESDAY 7

THURSDAY 8

FRIDAY 9 ★ Embraces intimate feelings in spite of any differences

---

SATURDAY 10 ★

SUNDAY 11 ★

MONDAY 12

TUESDAY 13 ●

WEDNESDAY 14

THURSDAY 15 ★ Earn your freedom one small step at a time

FRIDAY 16

SATURDAY 17

SUNDAY 18

MONDAY 19

TUESDAY 20

WEDNESDAY 21

THURSDAY 22 ★ **SUPER NOVA DAYS** Hopes and dreams override reality

---

FRIDAY 23 ★

SATURDAY 24

SUNDAY 25

MONDAY 26 ★ Express your originality

TUESDAY 27

WEDNESDAY 28 ○

THURSDAY 29

FRIDAY 30

BURIED TREASURE

Secrecy, power, and spiritual transformation lead you to the depths of your soul this month. You may experience moments of unpleasantness as you face hidden issues about trust and ethics. However, you have untapped resources that require a journey to the shadows of your psyche for extraction so you can bring them into the light. Cryptic Pluto, the mythological Lord of the Underworld, is stirring in the lair of your 12th House of Soul Consciousness to awaken desires and expose fears with several aspects to strategy-making outer planets. On **December 20**, visionary Jupiter makes its second quincunx to Pluto—the first was **July 18** and the last is on **March 29, 2013**—forcing you to edit your expectations. It's wise to make minor adjustments now to avoid major losses later. Fortunately, reliable Saturn forms a competent sextile with incisive Pluto on **December 26** to concentrate your focus and get you back on course for the New Year.

Eliminate unrewarding projects and patterns to make room for the fresh ideas inspired by capricious Uranus's forward shift on **December 13**. Your sights are raised by the inspirational Sagittarius New Moon in your 11th House of Hopes and Wishes. Empowering Mars provides further momentum for change when he moves into nonconformist Aquarius on the **25th**. Still, ambition is best managed prudently as the Sun enters traditional Capricorn, marking the Winter Solstice on **December 21**. Work-related matters may be dramatized by the security-conscious Cancer Full Moon in your 6th House of Employment on the **28th**. The Moon's opposition to provocative Pluto and square with irrepressible Uranus foments restlessness. Nevertheless, the Full Moon trines stable Saturn, supplying a balance of reason.

SATURDAY 1 ★ Your enthusiasm could be contagious

SUNDAY 2 ★

MONDAY 3

TUESDAY 4

WEDNESDAY 5

THURSDAY 6

FRIDAY 7 ★ Attraction to an unusual individual or activity can be risky

SATURDAY 8

SUNDAY 9

MONDAY 10

TUESDAY 11

WEDNESDAY 12

THURSDAY 13 ●

FRIDAY 14 ★ Experiment with new techniques to get things done

SATURDAY 15 ★

SUNDAY 16 ★

MONDAY 17

TUESDAY 18

WEDNESDAY 19 ★ You can have your cake and eat it, too

THURSDAY 20

FRIDAY 21

SATURDAY 22

SUNDAY 23

MONDAY 24

TUESDAY 25 ★ **SUPER NOVA DAYS** Start new traditions

WEDNESDAY 26 ★

THURSDAY 27

FRIDAY 28 ○

SATURDAY 29

SUNDAY 30

MONDAY 31

2013 HOROSCOPE

AQUARIUS

JANUARY 20–FEBRUARY 18

AQUARIUS 2013 OVERVIEW

You're caught in complexity this year, because revolutionary Uranus awakens your mind to fresh ideas and new ways to communicate as it continues to occupy your 3rd House of Information and Education. At the same time, however, a powerful series of squares between your ruling planet Uranus and potent Pluto that began last year pressures you to avoid taking risks and exploring unfamiliar territory. These contradictory aspects occur on May 20 and November 1 and complete this cycle of alignments on March 16, 2015. **Fortunately, if you're willing to face your fears, you could discover that some aren't real and that you can finally let them go.** Self-awareness is essential to recognizing the beliefs that stand between you and success, empowering you to eliminate unproductive attitudes from your life. You'll be ready to take action and break free from the past with the arrival of spring, for Uranus is joined by energetic Mars on March 22, by the Sun and Venus on March 28, and by perceptive Mercury on April 20. Even if you're unable to make a radical move during these chaotic times, you can catch glimpses of a more exciting future that's worth pursuing later.

Opportunities for personal growth abound as Jupiter visits your 5th House of Self-Expression, bringing out the playful kid in you. On June 25, visionary Jupiter enters your 6th House of Employment to increase opportunities for professional growth and add meaning to your work. **A strategic perspective allows you to step back from the daily grind to reassess your skills and determine how to apply them more effectively.** Greater efficiency in your current workplace is likely, but this new awareness of your abilities can also inspire you to seek additional training and aim for a more rewarding position. Wise Jupiter's presence in emotional Cancer awakens strong feelings about how you serve others. If you're stuck in a dull and lifeless situation, this transit triggers a desire to change your career trajectory. Security comes from following your highest instincts instead of fearfully holding on to a job that pays your salary but robs your soul.

Skepticism can close minds and cynicism

darkens hearts, yet tempering high hopes with a dash of doubt and humility will do wonders for you this year. Heavy-handed Saturn in scrutinizing Scorpio occupies your 10th House of Career and Public Life, weighing you down with extra responsibilities. Therefore, **a more discriminating sense of judgment helps you to avoid taking on obligations that aren't worth the time and effort required to fulfill them.** This comes in very handy when optimistic Jupiter squares impulsive Uranus on August 21 and you're tempted to take a giant leap without fully considering where you will land. Fortunately, you're given a more strategic perspective when well-balanced Jupiter-Saturn trines activate your work-related 6th and 10th Houses on July 17 and December 12, repeating on May 24, 2014, motivating you to make a serious career decision. Your assessment of where it's appropriate to expand and seek opportunities and what you must do to strengthen your skills to support these ambitions should be right on target.

FUN AND GAMES

Romantic Venus enters unconventional Aquarius and your 1st House of Self to enrich your personal life on February 1. Update your appearance and experiment in relationships; you'll garner plenty of attention and affection. Outgoing Jupiter occupies your 5th House of Love until June 25, which is bound to raise your social profile. Your capacity to have fun in a wide variety of circumstances might lead some people to take you less seriously. But this joyous way of acting doesn't reflect the deep thinker behind your playful smile. On August 6, the New Moon in bighearted Leo in your 7th House of Others forms a harmonious trine with eye-opening Uranus. Unexpected events and unusual people can lead to breakthroughs in your current alliance or spawn opportunities for exciting new connections.

WORK IN PROGRESS

Responsible Saturn's presence in passionate Scorpio and your 10th House of Career indicates the importance of being emotionally engaged in your job this year. But stress from too many tasks or lack of professional opportunities can squash the creativity that will help you professionally. Happily, buoyant Jupiter's entry into caring Cancer and your 6th House of Employment on June 25 should lift your spirits. Learning new skills or finally gaining recognition for the ones you already have should make your work more rewarding. Jupiter's transit encourages you to start or expand your own business as well, but it's important not to spread yourself too thin or grow too fast. A Solar Eclipse in your 10th House on November 3 is conjunct to constraining Saturn, which can slam the brakes on a major project, push you past the limits of your abilities, or even wear you down mentally or physically. Slowing down to take a long-term view of your aspirations enables you to cut your losses now so you can gain more later.

DREAMING FOR DOLLARS

Inspiration is key to maintaining your income this year as imaginative Neptune continues its long-term presence in your 2nd House of Money. Still, there's a risk of letting idealism go too far when introspective Mercury in intuitive Pisces is retrograde in your 2nd House on February 23–March 17. Revisiting old financial dreams distracts you from the reality of your current financial situation. Pay careful attention to economic matters to avoid making any expensive mistakes. Jupiter and Neptune, the traditional and modern rulers of your 2nd House, form an opportunistic trine on July 17, which fills you with newfound faith in yourself and awakens a vision of future prosperity. Managing expectations and providing a solid foundation to bring them down to earth could be critical when Jupiter and Neptune form fuzzy sesquisquares that can blur your judgment on September 28, December 17, and June 11, 2014.

SHOCK TO THE SYSTEM

It's tempting to ignore physical concerns while oppressive Pluto continues its long-lasting series of squares with irrepressible Uranus. Yet denying your body's needs could lead to an unpleasant surprise when overblown Jupiter squares Uranus on August 21. This is the first of three tense aspects that are meant to alert you to health concerns you might prefer to ignore. A radical shift in diet or exercise may be appealing, but it's better to make less dramatic modifications that you can stick with than to go to extremes that you won't sustain. Jupiter and Uranus will meet again on February 26 and April 20, 2014, indicating the importance of being flexible enough to respond quickly as you learn new ways to strengthen your immune system and improve your overall physical well-being.

REBUILD FROM THE GROUND UP

A Taurus Solar Eclipse in your 4th House of Domestic Conditions on May 9 shakes family traditions, destabilizes your home life, and forces you to reexamine your relationship to the past— potentially influencing your life for the next six months. Four planets in stubborn Taurus make change difficult as either you or someone close to you resists it. Core values may be at stake, which is why heels are dug in so deeply. Yet if you're willing to step out of outmoded emotional patterns and surrender old ways of thinking, the certainty that's lost will be richly compensated by the sense of freedom that you gain.

PLEASURE PRINCIPLE

It's a perfect time to embark on a trip when sensuous Venus, the ruler of your 9th House of Faraway Places, joins adventurous Jupiter on May 28. This cosmic union in your 5th House of Love and Play can inspire you to journey to an exotic locale. The artistic Libra New Moon on October 4 occurs in your 9th House, which may also spur you to dream of travel and enjoyable educational experiences. However, exigent Pluto's tense square to this Sun-Moon conjunction suggests that you should consider the hidden costs and personal risks before investing in a pricey excursion.

DIVINE INSPIRATION

Spiritual studies are interesting but won't affect your life as much as regular devotional practices. The Sun's presence in orderly Capricorn and your 12th House of Soul Consciousness when the year begins nourishes your soul with a regular routine of prayer, meditation, or communing with nature. Alluring Venus's union with transformational Pluto in your 12th House on January 16 may test your faith, yet rededicating yourself to a higher purpose empowers you to create positive change. Astonishing Uranus opens your eyes to a whole new universe of possibilities on May 20 and November 1, when it squares evolutionary Pluto.

RICK & JEFF'S TIP FOR THE YEAR
Agility Creates Options

Your incessant need to be right can get in the way of learning, growing, and discovering more effective ways to run your life. Recognizing that there are many different roads to happiness frees you from hanging on to impossible goals and unrealistic expectations. Adaptability, innovation, and exploration are more rewarding allies than persistence in the face of unyielding obstacles. When you run into walls, back up and look for ways to go around them instead of trying to knock them down.

JANUARY

WAITING IN THE WINGS

You start the year on an energetic note with dynamic Mars in Aquarius and your 1st House of Physicality, yet obtaining results and recognition for your efforts may not be easy at first. The Sun lurking in the shadows of your 12th House of Secrets until **January 19** makes it hard to get noticed. But you might like the privacy, as it may be more comfortable to work outside the glare of the spotlight. In fact, on **January 8** resourceful Venus shifts into well-organized Capricorn and your 12th House, suggesting that your most significant personal and professional encounters occur behind closed doors. Discretion in relationships is a must, since exposing intimate issues could be especially embarrassing now. The ambitious Capricorn New Moon on **January 11** can spur interest in big projects, but you have a great deal of preparation to do before you can go public with your plans. Completing unfinished business and increasing your efficiency must come first.

    Your personal New Year begins on **January 19** when brainy Mercury and the confidence-building

Sun enter Aquarius. A fresh wave of enthusiasm encourages you to get your body in shape and to start reaching out to more people. Your capacity to engage others in what you're doing expands with the growing force of your personality. The melodramatic Leo Full Moon in your 7th House of Partners on **January 26** forms a tense square with resistant Saturn. However, you can overcome delays, doubts, and denial from others with originality as farsighted Jupiter and progressive Uranus align favorably with this lunation to show you new solutions to old problems.

KEEP IN MIND THIS MONTH

Even your most brilliant ideas will fail if they're not rooted in an orderly life that gives you the freedom to take chances without losing your solid footing.

KEY DATES

SUPER NOVA DAYS

★ **JANUARY 3–7**

color between the lines

Expect surprising information to arrive—as
well as a sudden change of mind—with a
brilliant but volatile Mercury-Uranus square
on **January 3**. Don't overreact or respond
recklessly if your instinct to move quickly
is fired up by a high-energy trine between
impatient Mars and boundless Jupiter on
the **4th**. This supercharged alignment helps
you push your body and sell your ideas
with entrepreneurial fervor. But pesky
Mercury fakes you out on the **5th** with an
awkward quincunx to Jupiter that spawns
misstatements or prompts you to misconstrue
facts. The hammer of reality starts to fall when
Mercury joins incisive Pluto on **January 6**,
demanding concentration, exposing flaws,
and intensifying communication. The final
shot comes with a stern Mars-Saturn square
on the **7th** that allows no room for errors.
Accountability is high, especially at work, but

you can garner some hard-earned respect if
you demonstrate discipline and patience.

★ **JANUARY 12**
love interrupted
Affable Venus's square with strange Uranus
can upset a relationship with a sudden change
of moods, tastes, or plans. It's helpful to leave
yourself an exit strategy if you're not sure
that you want to stick to a social engagement.
Taking time to be alone or exploring
unconventional forms of fun are appropriate
ways to express this aspect.

★ **JANUARY 19–20**
velvet revolution
Your excitement rises when friendly Mercury
and the radiant Sun enter your sign on
January 19. You act impulsively with an
explosive Mars-Uranus semisquare on
the **20th** that can find you in a less-than-
cooperative mood. Inventing your own rules
and acting independently could upset others
unless you temper your behavior with a
spoonful of sweetness.

★ **JANUARY 24-25**
  back to the books
  You may be cooking up some new ideas
  with an ingenious Sun-Uranus sextile on
  January 24, allowing you to present an odd
  concept in ways that others can understand.
  Maintaining support, though, is challenging on
  the **25th** when Mercury forms a square with
  skeptical Saturn, leading people to doubt you
  or to demand proof that what you're saying is
  actually true. Don't force an issue; you may
  need to exercise self-restraint and do some
  further research to build a solid case.

★ **JANUARY 30**
  work now play later
  Joyful Jupiter's forward turn in your 5th House
  of Play on **January 30** is ready to unlock some
  chances for fun that have been on hold for
  too long. But you may have to wait patiently
  to cash in your golden ticket since a somber
  Sun-Saturn square dominates the day. Work
  responsibilities come first and require a level
  of commitment that doesn't allow much room
  for distraction.

FEBRUARY

FOLLOW YOUR BLISS

Money matters are on your mind as four planets move into quixotic Pisces and your 2nd House of Income this month. Action-planet Mars leads the way on **February 1**, followed by messenger Mercury on the **5th**, the Sun on the **18th**, and lucrative Venus on the **25th**. Economic issues are closely connected to your ideals; if your work aligns with your beliefs, the cash will flow more readily. But if you're stuck in an uninspiring job, being well paid will not be enough to keep you happy and healthy. Finding a higher purpose and putting more passion into what you do are well worth the effort; if that's impossible in your current situation, looking elsewhere is a good idea. You might find it easier to change directions now, because amicable Venus enters Aquarius and your 1st House of Self on **February 1** to make you more appealing to others. An image makeover gives you confidence that infuses your professional and personal lifes, adding to your charisma.

The intelligent Aquarius New Moon on **February 10** empowers you to tackle unfamiliar tasks and take the initiative in relationships. Quicksilver Mercury slips into reverse gear on the **23rd**, turning retrograde in your 2nd House of Resources, where it backpedals until **March 17**. Reviewing financial records could save you from some costly errors, and reminiscing about the past can revive interest in long-ignored talents. If you have been overpaying with money, commitment, love, or energy, the bill may come due with the exacting Virgo Full Moon that highlights your 8th House of Deep Sharing on **February 25**. It's time to closely examine what you're receiving from others and to restate your expectations as precisely as you can.

KEEP IN MIND THIS MONTH

The most practical moves for others won't necessarily benefit you. Trust your instincts before following someone else's advice.

KEY DATES

SUPER NOVA DAYS

★ **FEBRUARY 6–7**

irresistible you

Brains and personality are a tough
combination to beat—and you have both
working in your favor now. Charming
Venus's slick sextile to innovative Uranus on
February 6 enables you to lead people where
you want them to go and make them think it's
their idea. The imaginative power of cerebral
Mercury's conjunction with Neptune, the
fantasy planet, inspires you to paint beautiful
verbal pictures that help you iron out conflicts
with others. Smooth talking, however, is only
a temporary bridge to overcome differences,
so remember that you must fill in many details
before you can turn this dream into reality.
Still, a beautiful Venus-Jupiter trine on the **7th**
is astrology's most favorable aspect between
its two traditional "benefics." It's bound to
lift your spirits and show off your captivating
personality; people will have a hard time
refusing your requests. Don't spend all this

goodwill on trivial matters when you can gain
acceptance and even support that grows into
love and professional admiration.

★ **FEBRUARY 9–11**
patience is a virtue
Use your common sense on **February 9**, when
a rebellious Sun-Uranus semisquare can
trigger you to act impulsively. You may have
a brilliant new idea, but you tend to go too
far too fast with an overheated Mars-Jupiter
square on **January 10**. Being right isn't an
asset when your opinions are so strong that
they push others away or provoke you into
careless behavior. The quirky Aquarius New
Moon, also on the **10th**, marks the beginning
of a personal cycle of development. A serious
Venus-Saturn square on the **11th** can take
some air out of your social balloon, but it's
meant to encourage you to make careful
calculations before investing too much of
yourself. Don't try to race past your doubts;
you're more likely to find fulfillment when you
diligently work for it.

★ **FEBRUARY 15–16**
eye of the tiger
You feel physically strong and tremendously productive with two days of friction-free aspects involving muscular Mars. A sextile with powerful Pluto on **February 15** and trine with hardworking Saturn on the **16th** ensure concentration that permits you to operate at a very high level of efficiency.

★ **FEBRUARY 19–22**
change of heart
Relationships could go askew with flirty Venus's edgy semisquare to unruly Uranus on **February 19**. Your tastes may suddenly shift as the potential for boredom rises. It's best, though, to avoid playing games with those you love, because provocative Pluto's semisquare to Venus on the **22nd** can lure you across a line that permanently alters a partnership.

MARCH

THINK DIFFERENT

If you're a lover of new ideas—which most Aquarians are—you're in for an amazing month. Valiant Mars leads the way on **March 12** when he enters pioneering Aries and your 3rd House of Information and Education to fire up your brain with intellectual challenges. The Sun shifts into bold Aries on the **20th**, marking the Spring Equinox, to add confidence in your search for answers and inspire courage in your drive to express yourself. Sassy Venus makes the same transition on the **21st**, spicing up your conversations and learning experiences with flirtatious intrigue. Yet before you start indulging in pleasure, it pays to take another look at money matters, because the spacey Pisces New Moon falls in your 2nd House of Income on **March 11**. Conjunctions with aesthetic Venus and ardent Mars give you a boost of creativity to increase your cash flow, enhance your self-worth, and put more delight in your personal life.

It's time to leave financial fantasies behind and address current economic issues in a realistic manner when Mercury's direct turn in your 2nd

House of Finances on **March 17** occurs very close to dreamy Neptune. If you've had a moneymaking plan on hold, however, the messenger planet picks up speed in the weeks ahead, which could get your deal moving again. On **March 27**, the usually languorous Libra Full Moon in your 9th House of Faraway Places is agitated by hard aspects to Uranus, Pluto, Venus, and Mars that could shake up travel plans. A sudden impulse to change your itinerary or take off for an exotic locale can inspire your mind, but may be overly ambitious for your budget.

KEEP IN MIND THIS MONTH

If you can't apply an exciting insight in your life right now, let it go. Many more bright ideas will be coming your way.

KEY DATES

★ **MARCH 4**

money can't buy you love

An old financial scheme could reappear
with retrograde Mercury rejoining the Sun
in your 2nd House of Assets. However, it's
likely to look a lot better than it really is with
an overly optimistic square between value-
conscious Venus and opulent Jupiter. A small
expenditure of energy, hope, or money is an
inexpensive way to add more pleasure to your
life without locking yourself into a long-term
commitment that can prove very costly.

★ **MARCH 7-9**

cut to the chase

If you're in a jam on **March 7**, it makes sense
that you try to force a resolution to get out
of it, because pushy Mars is tangling with
stubborn Saturn. However, a brilliant Mars-
Jupiter quintile suggests that there are more
inventive ways to address the issue. Brains
definitely work better than brawn today. The
second of three profound but subtle sextiles

between constructive Saturn and productive Pluto on the **8th** reminds you to narrow your focus and concentrate on one task at a time. Hard work now can pay off later with their third and final sextile on **September 21**. Maintaining the discipline needed to follow through, though, may not be easy when Mercury's square to Jupiter on **March 9** scatters your attention in several directions.

SUPER NOVA DAY

★ MARCH 22
rebel without a cause

Electricity is in the air with fire-starter Mars joining high-frequency Uranus in combustible Aries. This bolt of energy rattles your 3rd House of Communication, awakening intuition and sparking instantaneous reactions. You could release this energy through misdirected anger, rebellious refusal to follow the rules— or sudden enlightenment. Warrior Mars hooking up with radical Uranus is a fight for freedom, but you're not the only one feeling it, which can cause conflict on all fronts. Trying your hand at new experiences puts you in sync with this aspect, but a dash of detachment is needed to avoid an emotional meltdown.

★ MARCH 26
no guts, no glory
Go-getter Mars's ambitious sextile with gigantic Jupiter encourages you to express yourself more energetically, which is fabulous for making your point. Yet Mars's square with unforgiving Pluto punishes imprecision, so don't promise more than you can deliver.

★ MARCH 28
chemical attraction
You find wondrous things around every corner when delectable Venus joins the heartfelt Sun and extraterrestrial Uranus to delight your senses in unexpected ways. Your tastes are turned upside down as delicious new flavors of people and experiences offer surprising forms of joy. Love at first sight, touch, or smell can excite you in an instant . . . but could be so fleeting that it does not last the day.

APRIL

STOP, LOOK, AND LISTEN

You can charm the birds right out of the trees this month with several planets rolling through enthusiastic Aries and your 3rd House of Communication. And even if you don't get what you want, you'll have a lot of fun trying. The pioneering Aries New Moon lands in this chatty part of your chart on **April 10**, hooking up with creative lovers Venus and Mars to put a twinkle in your eye and a sparkle in your speech, making this a great time to jump into an artistic project. Your capacity for pleasure grows, and lively connections with others should come easily. However, a more sobering moment arrives when strict Saturn forms a corrective quincunx to independent Uranus on the **12th**. This aspect first occurred on **November 15, 2012**, possibly derailing an original plan or a break for freedom. It's time to adjust your course so that you can keep the essence of a revolutionary idea instead of having it completely fall apart with the final Saturn-Uranus quincunx on **October 5**.

Your thinking speeds up when quick-witted Mercury zips into fast-moving Aries on **April 13**, but lovable Venus ambles into leisurely Taurus and your domestic 4th House on the **15th** to slow things down at home. Taking time to explore sensual delights and beautify your environment enriches your life. While you continue to sizzle with hot new ideas, the shifts of the Sun and Mars into Taurus on the **19th** and **20th** are not-so-subtle reminders to pace yourself. Caution is also called for on **April 25** when the emotionally intense Scorpio Full Moon Eclipse joins ethical Saturn in your 10th House of Career, challenging you to face the music and make a major decision in your professional life.

KEEP IN MIND THIS MONTH

No matter how quickly your brain races, slow down to consider your options. Besides, taking the scenic route provides delight you won't find in the fast lane.

KEY DATES

★ **APRIL 1**
courage of your convictions
There's no fooling you today as wise Jupiter
aligns in a smart sextile with the Sun. Your
voice will be heard, and your high ideals can
inspire others. Creativity also pops with this
harmonious aspect since the bold Sun is
illuminating your 3rd House of Communication
and Jupiter is expanding your 5th House of
Self-Expression.

★ **APRIL 6–7**
tunnel of love
Believing in illusions is tempting as insistent
Mars and enchanting Venus form anxious
semisquares with surreal Neptune on **April 6**.
Romantic fantasies and artistic flights of
fancy are wonderful, but don't bet your
heart or spend your money on anything less
than a sure thing. The urgency to jump into
someone's arms or into an irresistible project
intensifies with a Venus-Mars conjunction
on the **7th**. The heat of your enthusiasm is

palpable and encourages you to take risks
both personally and professionally. Just
consider this a test drive instead of a long-
term commitment.

★ **APRIL 14**
know your limits
You're enchanted with what others have to
offer today—but it may sound better than it
really is. Appreciative Venus in excitable Aries
makes an errant semisquare with generous
Jupiter, which often leads to overestimating
people or inflating the worth of an experience.
The Moon joins Jupiter in your 5th House of
Fun and Games in fast-talking Gemini and can
entice you into a playful activity before you
consider the consequences. Pushing the limits
of pleasure and creativity is a good idea as
long as you don't go to extremes.

★ **APRIL 17**
hit the ground running
The Sun joins contentious Mars in your
conversational 3rd House where it can easily
provoke arguments. Uncontainable impatience

and excessive certainty about one's ideas are
the likely triggers of verbal sparring. If you
have a point, make it and move on instead
of getting bogged down in a petty dispute.
However, if you can apply the passion you're
feeling to create a meaningful connection with
someone you admire or begin a fascinating
new course of study, the powerful fire of this
conjunction propels you in an exciting new
direction.

SUPER NOVA DAYS

★ **APRIL 20–22**
genius at work
Your ability to think outside the box can lead
to breakthroughs in awareness on **April 20**,
thanks to the intellectual electricity of an
incandescent but nervous Mercury-Uranus
conjunction. Still, you must remain patient and
pragmatic with Mercury's square to exacting
Pluto on the **21st**. Purging unessential
information reveals what's most important,
which can earn you trust from others when
Venus opposes stern Saturn on the **22nd**.

MAY

THE CHOICE IS YOURS

A pair of powerful eclipses leads you to reconsider long-term goals this month. On **May 9**, a conventional Taurus Solar Eclipse in your 4th House of Roots may cause you to take a step back from a home-based project or address a family matter that you thought was already settled. It's crucial that you firm up your foundation with a visionary Sagittarius Full Moon Lunar Eclipse in your 11th House of Dreams and Wishes on **May 25**. Illusory Neptune's stressful square to the eclipse might attract you to an unrealizable goal or inspire you to invest more in a project that's already draining your resources. It's best to unburden yourself of unnecessary obligations, especially with the earthshaking Uranus-Pluto square on the **20th**. Save your strength to deal with unexpected emergencies or sudden opportunities that require your attention.

Your thoughts about the future may be nourished with new information this month—or overstuffed with choices that complicate decision making. Vivacious Venus, curious Mercury, the willful Sun, and hyperactive Mars enter diverse

Gemini and your 9th House of Higher Thought and Faraway Places on **May 9, 15, 20,** and **31**, respectively, presenting you with more options than you have time to explore. Your attraction to a variety of belief systems and distant cultures is enormously entertaining and educational but is likely to distract you from the real work of your daily life. It's time for you to choose one direction on **May 20**, with dispersive Jupiter's third and final sesquisquare to steadfast Saturn. Commit yourself to one major goal by gathering your attention and pointing it in a singular direction. Doing so will advance your ambitions; failing to can keep you stuck where you are.

KEEP IN MIND THIS MONTH

Recognizing the difference between a passing interest and an enduring passion will help you to stop flirting with plans that have little likelihood of fulfillment.

KEY DATES

★ **MAY 1**

no pain, no gain

Conflicting obligations at home and work can put you in a pressure-packed situation. An opposition between active Mars in your 4th House of Domestic Conditions and exigent Saturn in your 10th House of Profession can leave you feeling hemmed in and, perhaps, frustrated by all that's demanded of you. The good news is that all this stress could cause you to clarify your priorities and establish a more disciplined approach or a better system, becoming more effective in both places.

★ **MAY 5–6**

agent of change

Expect surprises in your personal life on **May 5** when loving Venus misaligns with unsettling Uranus. Irrational behavior and irresponsible people can rattle your relationships. You may be exhilarated to discover newfound freedom and forms of fun, but you're more likely to feel uncomfortable. If you go out on a limb, primal

Pluto's connection with Venus on the **6th** will either break it off or pull you back down to the ground. You could meet the consequences of carelessness, yet you might also realize that altering the nature of your partnerships is worth whatever price you have to pay.

★ **MAY 16–18**
call of the wild
An anti-authoritarian Sun-Uranus semisquare on **May 16** could put you in an uncooperative mood. Dealing with bosses and bossy people more than you like stirs you up enough to rebel. Still, following your own path might spur you to create innovative methods that put your individuality in a favorable light. Happily, even if you go too far, an open-minded Venus-Uranus sextile on the **18th** earns acceptance for your unconventional ways. You'll find it easier to let go of the past and live more freely in the present.

★ **MAY 20**
stroke of genius
If you're faced with a difficult problem today, thinking it through can pay off with

an illuminating breakthrough when Uranus squares Pluto. Thoughtful Mercury's quincunx with compelling Pluto runs you into a wall of doubt or a frustrating conversation. However, Mercury's subsequent sextile to liberating Uranus awakens you with an epiphany that helps you discover an unexpected solution to this impasse.

SUPER NOVA DAYS

★ **MAY 26–28**

give peace a chance

An uncompromising Mars-Uranus semisquare on **May 26** can spark a surprising conflict. Your unwillingness to meet others halfway could be genius or folly, but might alienate people either way. Philosophical Jupiter's conjunctions with mental Mercury on the **27th** and diplomatic Venus on the **28th** arm you with insights and information that can resolve a sticky situation. Your willingness to see all sides of an issue restores intellectual and emotional connections.

JUNE

LIVING IN THE MATERIAL WORLD

Strong feelings about your job tempt you to push logic aside this month and get in touch with your deeper needs regarding your professional life. Vulnerable Venus shifts into security-seeking Cancer and your 6th House of Employment on **June 2** to bring personal matters into the workplace. Overly sensitive colleagues and customers could seem more demanding, but it's your inner needs that have to be addressed first. Still, the New Moon in friendly but noncommittal Gemini occurs in your 5th House of Romance on **June 8th**, offering numerous distractions from serious issues. On the plus side, you could be crackling with creativity and flirting with everyone you meet. Nevertheless, don't allow superficial interests to tempt you to take your eye off the ball.

On **June 11**, your attention turns to your highest economic dreams with the harmonious trine between constructive Saturn in your 10th House of Career and idealistic Neptune in your 2nd House of Resources. Focusing on your strategy for reaching these goals now will put you in a stronger position to make this happen when this trine recurs on **July 19**. Your vocational aspirations are illuminated by the Sun's shift into Cancer and your 6th House of Employment on **June 21**, marking the Summer Solstice. The well-organized Capricorn Full Moon on the **23rd** forms a supportive sextile with Saturn, making this an excellent time to complete unfinished tasks. It brightens your 12th House of Inner Peace, inviting you to commit to a regular spiritual practice. Although Jupiter begins a yearlong visit to your 6th House on the **25th**, helping you integrate your metaphysical interests into your daily routine, Mercury's retrograde turn on the **26th** buys you time to reflect on the past before moving forward.

KEEP IN MIND THIS MONTH

Don't set aside emotions just because they're uncomfortable or irrational. You can only find satisfaction if you acknowledge the deeper meaning behind your feelings.

KEY DATES

★ **JUNE 1**
leader of the pack
You get off to an awkward start today, seeing
any outside influence as undue pressure
thanks to the tunnel vision of a Sun-Pluto
quincunx. But the stress is relieved with a
solar sextile to surprising Uranus that allows
you to leap over earlier resistance with a
radically new perspective. Your sparkling
ideas and magnetic personality enable
you to enlighten others about the need for
personal freedom and the possibility of finding
alternative ways to get along.

★ **JUNE 7-8**
embrace the unknown
Amorous Venus's harmonious hook-ups
with compassionate Neptune and practical
Saturn bring balance to public and private
relationships on **June 7**. But restraint is
recommended as impetuous Mars squares
delusional Neptune, enticing you to chase
illusions instead of acting rationally. Although

the Gemini New Moon on the **8th** scatters
your energy, Mars skids into a quincunx with
Saturn, bringing down the hammer of reality.
Instead of being caught between a rock and
a hard place, an inventive Mercury-Uranus
square shatters your operating paradigm and
opens up new worlds of possibilities.

★ **JUNE 12**
occupational hazard
Be flexible on the job today when sociable
Venus in your 6th House of Service crashes
into a volatile square with unpredictable
Uranus. You may be confronted by unexpected
events and unusual individuals, or find that
you're easily bored by routine tasks. Yet
adapting quickly to situations could produce
excitement that elevates your interest in
others and in your work.

SUPER NOVA DAYS

★ **JUNE 17–19**
consider your audience
You're firing on all cylinders as two powerful
planetary aspects fuel you with energy and

enthusiasm. Initiating Mars's smart sextile to irrepressible Uranus on **June 17** excites you with creativity that ignites fresh opportunities and outflanks old obstacles. The beat goes on when the Sun joins limitless Jupiter in your 5th House of Love and Play on the **19th**. You're still effervescent with excitement, which makes you a powerful presenter of whatever you want to sell. Just be sure not to overwhelm your listener with every last bit of information because it's easier to get what you want when you don't clutter the conversation with extraneous details.

★ **JUNE 27–28**
star of the show
You're in the spotlight on **June 27** as Venus prances into bold and brassy Leo and your 7th House of Relationships. Expressing yourself openly is a risk worth taking. Still, don't rush or bite off more than you can chew on the **28th**, when conservative Saturn's constraining aspect to incorrigible Mars rewards patience and punishes haste.

JULY

ROOM AT THE TOP

In a life overflowing with fascinating ideas, you're not always able to find a viable one and stick to it, Aquarius—but that's exactly what you can do this month. Crystallizing Saturn turns direct in your 10th House of Profession on **July 8**, which prompts you to clarify current issues and career objectives. On the **17th**, enthusiastic Jupiter in your 6th House of Employment creates a Grand Water Trine with strategic Saturn and imaginative Neptune that helps you formalize a successful plan for advancing your interests. However, these ambitions may fail unless they're aligned with your highest ideals as Neptune occupies your 12th House of Spirituality. The nurturing Cancer New Moon lands in your 6th House on **July 8**, indicating changes at the workplace since challenging aspects to this lunation from evolutionary Pluto and shocking Uranus are bound to shake up the status quo. Consider a radical shift in your professional trajectory. You have the drive to learn new skills when physical Mars enters tenacious Cancer on the **13th** to put more passion into your daily activities.

The Winged Messenger makes a forward shift in your 6th House of Daily Routines on **July 20**, easing the communication that was stalled during Mercury's retrograde period beginning on **June 26**. Take a more rational approach to personal and professional partnerships when valuable Venus enters analytical Virgo and your 8th House of Deep Sharing on **July 22**. You may be dealing with picky people, or find yourself becoming more critical of others. The need to balance your desires in a relationship is underscored on the **22nd** by the Aquarius Full Moon's opposition to the dramatic Leo Sun in your 7th House of Partners.

KEEP IN MIND THIS MONTH

Innumerable little issues require your attention this month, but save the majority of your time for thinking about major long-term goals.

KEY DATES

★ **JULY 1**
hard to please
You're less than satisfied with how people are treating you today. It's due to Venus in prideful Leo moving from a restricting square with Saturn to a confusing quincunx with Neptune. You might feel underappreciated or choose to avoid an unpleasant individual. However, this is also a chance to redefine your expectations of others and then make compromises when necessary.

★ **JULY 4–7**
flags of freedom
These are exciting days that are kicked off by a cage-rattling Sun-Uranus square on **July 4** that provokes you to rebel against rules and tradition. Sweet Venus is jostled by sexy Mars and stressed by suspicious Pluto on the **5th**, which can undermine trust but can also intensify your desires. Happily, you can resolve conflicts with help from a supportive Venus-Uranus trine on the **7th**. Taking a new approach

to a complicated relationship feels like a fresh start, allowing you to let go of the past to create a more harmonious yet stimulating future.

★ **JULY 17–20**
dare to believe
Your workplace abounds with opportunities when giant Jupiter forms a Grand Water Trine with Saturn and Neptune on **July 17**. The strategic Saturn-Neptune trine on the **19th** puts your dreams within reach. However, partnerships continue to challenge you as innocent Venus tangles with manipulative Pluto on **July 18** and unstable Uranus on the **20th**. You risk extreme reactions as your resistance to being controlled is activated. But there are benefits to these disruptive patterns: You might drop people from your life who can't meet your needs, as well as discovering new sources of joy.

SUPER NOVA DAY

★ **JULY 22**
mixed messages
Caution is stressed when modest Venus minces into meticulous Virgo, but the Sun

boldly strides into flamboyant Leo and your 7th House of Partners, encouraging you to take chances with others. Meanwhile, the nonconformist Aquarius Full Moon suggests that breaking into unfamiliar territory requires a greater degree of self-mastery. Serious Saturn's square to this lunation picks up Venus's current theme of being reasonable and responsible, which is what it takes to be assertive without losing credibility or self-control.

★ **JULY 31**
mad genius
If your life feels like a delicate balancing act between responding logically and following your impulses, your wilder side is likely to tilt the scales today. An explosive Mars-Uranus square can trigger instantaneous reactions that are less than reasonable. Blowing up at someone or steaming with silent anger is not the best way to apply this energetic firestorm. Inventing original ways to manage tasks, though, can produce brilliant results.

AUGUST

DIPLOMATIC MEASURES

Relationships are front and center this month with the New and Full Moons activating your socially oriented 1st and 7th Houses. On **August 6**, the self-confident Leo New Moon lands in your 7th House of Partners, which widens the field for finding creative personal and professional alliances. Uncontainable Uranus's favorable trine to this lunation spurs breakthroughs in current unions and shows you unusual ways to make new friends. Expect strong emotions and increased sensitivity on **August 20** when the brilliant Aquarius Full Moon illuminates your 1st House of Self. You can easily enchant others, since mystical Neptune conjuncts this lunation. You may wander off into fantasyland and fail to see individuals you meet as they really are, but being more forgiving and sympathetic is a healthier expression of this pattern.

Battles over beliefs could break out with the first of three oppositions between opinionated Jupiter and propagandist Pluto on **August 7**. Don't lock yourself into a fixed position; Jupiter's square with unexpected Uranus on the **21st** can suddenly shift your point of view. The philosophical and strategic issues triggered by these transits won't settle until their final aspects on **April 20, 2014**. You'll enjoy better relations with intellectual adversaries, though, with Venus's entry into diplomatic Libra and your 9th House of Higher Mind on **August 16**. However, principles give way to pragmatism as the Sun and Mercury enter earthy Virgo and your 8th House of Intimacy on the **22nd** and **23rd**. Picking through the details of relationships can seem tedious and petty, but this planetary shift suggests that the future success of important partnerships requires careful analysis of your mutual needs and expectations.

KEEP IN MIND THIS MONTH

Being flexible enough to adjust from making plans for the future to addressing the nuts and bolts of the present is essential for creating more effective alliances.

KEY DATES

SUPER NOVA DAYS

★ **AUGUST 1–4**
reversal of fortune
On **August 1**, a pair of persnickety quincunxes could put you on edge. Power struggles are stirred by the Sun's irritating misalignment with Pluto, and social unease accompanies Venus's uncomfortable connection with Uranus. But better news follows on the **2nd**, when graceful Venus's smooth sextile to bold Mars provides the charm and social skills you need to transform awkward moments into playful or romantic ones. The thrilling Sun-Uranus trine on the **4th** offers you the chance to maintain your freedom of expression while collaborating with a brilliant partner.

★ **AUGUST 11–14**
jumbled wires
Think clearly, speak slowly, and remain patient on **August 11** in order to get your message across. Communications grow complicated when verbal Mercury is delayed by a square

with demanding Saturn. A similar struggle is possible on the **13th** when Mercury quincunxes enigmatic Pluto, which could darken conversations with mistrust. An ingenious Mercury-Uranus trine on the **14th** helps you leap over these obstacles and enliven dialogues with unconventional thoughts.

★ **AUGUST 19–20**
reconcilable differences
The Sun's hard aspects to Jupiter in sentimental Cancer and futuristic Uranus in pioneering Aries on **August 19** pull you between two very different views of reality. Unsettled feelings and persistent uncertainty suggest that this is a less-than-ideal time to make a major decision. The Aquarius Full Moon on the **20th** could result in a sudden illumination that shows you how to reconcile the seemingly contradictory needs for stimulation and safety.

★ **AUGUST 22**
free your mind
Nervous energy and intellectual restlessness could be high as cerebral Mercury forms

stressful angles with electrifying Uranus and judgmental Jupiter. Concentration is difficult when the flow of information is constantly interrupted. Yet if you can relax enough to remain flexible and open-minded, exciting discoveries offer unexpected answers and create surprising new connections.

★ **AUGUST 27**
fools rush in
You could be in the mood to party, but opportunities at work challenge you to find the time for it. Nevertheless, sensual Venus's over-the-top square with bountiful Jupiter in your 6th House of Employment encourages you to seek pleasure and approval that might cost more than you think. You're likely to overpay for things or overestimate the value of other people. Macho Mars moves into theatrical Leo and your 7th House of Partners, motivating you to fall madly in love or attempt to dazzle potential business allies. This dynamic planet will continue to embolden your actions until **October 15**, so pace yourself rather than trying to force something to happen too soon.

SEPTEMBER

COLLABORATIVE EFFORTS

Taking care of unsettled relationship business is your top priority this month. Avoid the temptation to assume that personal and professional partners are on the same page as you—because there's a good chance they're not. The discerning Virgo New Moon falls in your 8th House of Deep Sharing on **September 5** to bring your attention to the effectiveness of your alliances. Visionary Jupiter's smart sextile to this lunation shows you how your long-term goals resonate with the methods and routines you currently have in place. You may feel picky being more specific about what you need from others, but you must weave a tighter web of cooperation to achieve your highest potential. Perceptive Mercury's move into objective Libra and your 9th House of Higher Truth on the **9th** opens your eyes to opposing points of view, which should facilitate negotiations of all kinds.

You learn to extract more value from your working relationships on **September 11**, when Venus enters shrewd Scorpio and your 10th House of Career. Money matters are on your radar with the psychic Pisces Full Moon brightening your 2nd House of Finances on the **19th**. The presence of this lunation in your imaginative sign is a reminder that faith, idealism, and creativity are among your major economic assets. Your professional productivity rises with dutiful Saturn's third and final sextile with Pluto on the **21st**. What you did during their first two aspects on **December 26, 2012**, and **March 8** will likely determine how successful you are now. The Autumn Equinox occurs when the Sun shifts into lovely Libra and your 9th House of Travel and Education on the **22nd**, giving you an itch for adventure and learning.

KEEP IN MIND THIS MONTH

Criticism is helpful when it's constructive; share your comments with kindness and listen carefully when others have advice for you.

KEY DATES

★ **SEPTEMBER 2-4**
stay on track
Small differences provoke arguments when mouthy Mercury semisquares cranky Mars on **September 2**. Stick to the subject if you want results, because a slippery Mars-Neptune quincunx prompts you to fire verbal arrows in the wrong direction. You'll want to focus on real issues in a more rational manner when Mercury semisquares responsible Saturn on the **4th**. Patiently handling one specific problem at a time is more likely to produce a useful outcome than turning this into a philosophical debate.

★ **SEPTEMBER 9-11**
reality check
You may have to slam on the brakes to stop someone from pushing you too hard or demanding too much as forceful Mars is stifled by a square to restrictive Saturn on **September 9**. You could see a setback at work—or simply a lack of progress—although narrowing your focus to address one tough

task can earn you respect. Be prepared to
pare back or drop a project, especially when
purging Pluto quincunxes Mars on the **11th**.

SUPER NOVA DAYS

★ **SEPTEMBER 14–16**
ahead of the curve

An inspirational Venus-Neptune trine on
September 14 tempts you with sweet visions of
romance. A Mercury-Pluto square could bring
criticism that undermines your dreams, but an
inventive Mars-Uranus trine prompts creative
actions that allow you to leap over doubts
with a radically different way of getting things
done. A Mercury-Uranus opposition on the
16th stimulates unconventional thinking that
shakes previous connections. Your ideas may
be too far ahead of the times, requiring you to
simplify them or keep them to yourself to avoid
causing confusion.

★ **SEPTEMBER 19**
deluge of details

More is not necessarily merrier when it comes
to ideas, information, and input from others.

An overload of data accompanies the watery Pisces Full Moon and long-winded Mercury's tense square to bombastic Jupiter. Watch out for exaggerating your motives and making a mountain out of a molehill. On the other hand, if you can stretch your mind to include both intellectual and emotional truths, your awareness will grow and your capacity to educate and influence people will increase.

★ SEPTEMBER 26-28
luck of the draw

You earn recognition for your work on **September 26** with a favorable trine between admirable Venus in your 10th House of Career and auspicious Jupiter in your 6th House of Service. Jupiter's sesquisquare to serene Neptune on the **28th** enables you to use your imagination to convince others that you're on the right track. Enjoying the company of colleagues, material rewards, and emotional satisfaction in your job are all high on your agenda. But Venus's challenging square with reckless Mars intensifies relationships in ways that may be sexy, but might also create conflict.

OCTOBER

PUSH THE ENVELOPE

Your keen intelligence normally gives you a higher-than-average degree of certainty about what you know. A couple of key events this month, however, may raise questions for which you don't have the answers. The Libra New Moon in your 9th House of Big Ideas on **October 4** is bent by stressful squares to Pluto and Jupiter and shocked by an incendiary opposition to Uranus. While the upside could be the sudden revelation of the meaning of life—or at least of your life— you're more likely to see your perspective on the future shaken and stirred. If you're able to let go of old concepts, you could receive a heavy download of useful insights. Adaptability is also a must with the last of three Saturn-Uranus quincunxes happening on the **5th**. This oil-and-water mix of duty and freedom occurred on **November 15, 2012**, and **April 12**, throwing you curveballs that you can finally hit out of the park.

The impulsive Aries Lunar Eclipse on **October 18** falls in your 3rd House of Information, interrupting patterns of communication and learning. If you've rushed into a class or a relationship too quickly, you may need to go back and fill in some critical details before you can get back in gear. Trickster Mercury's switch from forward to reverse on **October 21** takes this theme of tying up loose ends to the next level. The messenger planet is retrograde in your 10th House of Career until **November 10**, possibly hindering professional activities with delays and miscommunications. This is your chance to do some serious research, reconnect with people from the past, and prepare for a new project at work.

KEEP IN MIND THIS MONTH

Your natural curiosity and genuine desire to learn make it easy for you to move on from outmoded ideas and discover new ones that work.

KEY DATES

SUPER NOVA DAYS

★ **OCTOBER 1–3**
sink or swim

Expect disagreements over matters of principle on **October 1** with the willful Sun in your 9th House of Higher Truth, creating a harsh square to controlling Pluto. This struggle could become personal on the **2nd** when needy Venus semisquares Pluto, encouraging you to examine your values and assess your resources. On the **3rd**, Venus and the Sun run into trouble with maverick Uranus, rattling personal relationships and professional alliances. Your chances of making discoveries and avoiding chaos improve when you and those around you are open to change.

★ **OCTOBER 7–8**
ready to rumble

There's an intense buzz in the air on **October 7** as combative Mars in your 7th House of Partners clashes with wayward Uranus, provoking rebellious and impetuous behavior.

Cooperation eludes you as the desire to do things your own way or the challenge of dealing with an unreliable individual keeps you on edge. Intellectual Mercury's quincunx with Uranus on the **8th** adds more static, confusion, and crankiness. However, the messenger planet joins strict Saturn to set some requirements for logic, order, and accountability in your life.

★ **OCTOBER 16**
fearless leader

You may gain the enthusiastic support of others with enticing Venus in your 11th House of Groups creating a thrilling trine with trendsetting Uranus. You respond eagerly to unconventional sources of fun and are willing to try an irreverent approach to overcome obstacles in relationships. Experimenting with new ways of working with others could produce surprisingly positive results.

★ **OCTOBER 24–25**
the audacity of hope

Mars in fussy Virgo forms an expansive semi-square with Jupiter on **October 24** that can entangle you in a never-ending task. Before you embark on a new project or a complex negotiation, set parameters about how much you're willing to invest. Frustration may trigger criticism that weakens an important relationship. Forgiving and letting go come easily on the **25th**, when the Sun forms a generous trine with ethereal Neptune. Faith, creativity, and camaraderie flow freely, especially with those who share your altruistic ideals.

★ OCTOBER 31
the edge of glory
Unexpected circumstances are likely to shift even the most carefully crafted agenda. A potent and purposeful Mars-Pluto trine would normally make this a very productive time. Eliminating unnecessary people, things, and activities is meant to make you more efficient and not to hurt anyone's feelings. However, Mars's quincunx with quirky Uranus tosses a monkey wrench in your plans. Be prepared to adjust your approach to resolve an issue by using unconventional means or surprising tactics.

NOVEMBER

CLAIM YOUR POWER

You could be facing heavy issues in your professional life this month, with significant activity in your 10th House of Career. The action starts with a jolt of energy on **November 1** from the transformational Uranus-Pluto square. If you're dissatisfied with your job, it's smarter to look in other directions than to just quit and walk away. The potent Scorpio New Moon Solar Eclipse in your 10th House on **November 3** could have a profound effect on your future. A karmic Saturn conjunct to this eclipse indicates an overload of responsibilities, growing frustrations, or hard-earned accomplishments. Supportive aspects from unstoppable Mars and formidable Pluto add the punch you need to ride out the storm or, better yet, fuel your desire to move in a more fulfilling direction. There's little advantage to playing your hand openly now as pleasure-seeking Venus rewards discretion when it slips into the shadows of your 12th House of Privacy on the **5th**.

Opportunistic Jupiter's retrograde shift in your 6th House of Work on **November 7** points you toward the past for inspiration about your vocational choices. Data-driven Mercury's forward turn in your 10th House on **November 10** sets information flowing more freely. Domestic issues are in the spotlight when the steady Taurus Full Moon on the **17th** illuminates your 4th House of Roots. This is a signal to stop and smell the roses at home regardless of how demanding your job might be now. Making your environment more comfortable and spending time with those closest to you solidifies your emotional and physical foundations. The Sun shoots into adventurous Sagittarius and lights up your 11th House of Teamwork on **November 21**, encouraging you to connect more with friends, groups, and organizations.

KEEP IN MIND THIS MONTH

Take your time with a key career-related matter because the quickest solution may not be the most beneficial one in the long run.

KEY DATES

★ **NOVEMBER 6**
trust your instincts

Constrictive Saturn joins the expressive Sun
in your 10th House of Profession, presenting
a challenge that requires both patience and
leadership skills. It's wise to avoid making
any hasty moves; the impact of your actions
may be greater than you anticipate. Difficulties
with an authority figure or with your own
leadership style are possible. Delays and self-
doubt could cause you to question your job
performance. But don't rely on intellect alone,
because this conjunction in watery Scorpio
demands emotional awareness if you're to
manage stressful situations successfully.

★ **NOVEMBER 12**
lucky streak

Your capacity for recognizing others' needs
and abilities allows you to sell ideas today and
inspire people to follow your lead. Fortuitous
Jupiter's supportive trine to the Sun in your
10th House of Public Responsibility increases

on-the-job optimism, broadens your vision, and expands your professional base. Once again, the answers you seek are not just in your head, but need to correspond with your instincts. It's good strategy to take calculated risks on this propitious day.

SUPER NOVA DAYS

★ **NOVEMBER 14–16**
rocking the free world

Feelings that you've been keeping to yourself may pop out unexpectedly on **November 14**. Social Venus's kinetic square with volatile Uranus may provoke you to reveal a secret or wake up to a hidden truth about your own desires. But your liberated feelings may not last long, because Venus is squeezed by a hookup with mysterious Pluto on the **15th** that reveals deeper layers of meaning. You could be going on a relationship roller-coaster ride, especially with the Sun forming challenging aspects with both Uranus and Pluto on the **16th**. The benefits of these potentially upsetting alignments include discovering unique sources of pleasure, uncovering

unexpressed talents, and breaking free of
unrewarding alliances and responsibilities.

★ **NOVEMBER 25**
singular focus
Analytical Mercury's conjunction with unyielding
Saturn might impede communication.
Concentrate your attention on the single most
important issue of the day. While operating
within these narrow confines isn't fun, the extra
attention you give to a critical matter could
enable you to solve the problem once and for all.

★ **NOVEMBER 30**
free at last
You could be nervous enough to interrupt
conversations today with a sketchy Mercury-
Uranus sesquisquare. Yet you should be able
to turn the strange perceptions this triggers
into useful information. The Sun's creative
trine to wild Uranus frees you to express
yourself more openly. Collaborating with
forward-thinking individuals makes new social
experiences more exciting and also ignites
brilliant ideas that serve a cause or group.

DECEMBER

KEEP THE FAITH

Your role in the community is especially important this month with a good deal of planetary activity happening in your 11th House of Social Networking, starting with the high-spirited Sagittarius New Moon on **December 2**. This inspirational lunation cultivates friendships, initiates group activities, and encourages you to be a more enthusiastic teammate. Unorthodox Uranus's favorable trine to this Sun-Moon conjunction can reinvigorate your interest in an organization. Verbose Mercury blasts into Sagittarius on the **4th**, bringing bigger ideas and more contacts to the table—but possibly carrying you away with impractical beliefs. Warrior Mars turns peaceful in cooperative Libra on **December 7** as it enters your 9th House of Faraway Places. Advocating for the truth often creates conflict, yet now you may be able to do it graciously enough to maintain civil conversations with those who don't agree with you.

You have a solid grasp of your professional ambitions on **December 12** with the second of three strategically sound Jupiter-Saturn trines.

You might reassess goals that came with their first trine on **July 17** and make adjustments to them that could bear fruit with their final recurrence on **May 24, 2014**. A flirtatious Gemini Full Moon on **December 17** charges your 5th House of Self-Expression, prompting playful, creative, and even romantic impulses. The metaphysical Jupiter-Neptune sesquisquare amplifies your holiday spirit, while retrograde Uranus turns forward the same day, releasing energy that increases your taste for freedom. The Sun's shift into traditional Capricorn on **December 21** marks the Winter Solstice while heart-centered Venus turns retrograde in your 12th House of Divinity, reviving old questions about the purpose of life. Thankfully, clever Mercury's move into Capricorn on the **24th** just might give you some of the answers you seek.

KEEP IN MIND THIS MONTH

Instead of following familiar traditions throughout the holiday season, shake things up. Dynamic times call for you to embrace change.

KEY DATES

★ **DECEMBER 6–7**
lost in space
Your mind can float off to some interesting places with a surreal Mercury-Neptune square on **December 6**. Your creativity is off the charts, but so is the potential for confusion, cloudy thinking, and miscommunication. Yet pushing your point or trying to get the clarity you need from others may not be easy when Mercury forms an overstated sesquisquare with outlandish Jupiter on the **7th**. Facts remain fuzzy, so take what you hear with a grain of salt.

★ **DECEMBER 10**
in the zone
You're working with your full arsenal of intelligence and ingenuity today when a brilliant Mercury-Uranus trine enhances your intuition, emboldening you to contribute original ideas that can be immediately useful. Your keen sense of people and economic acuity are also heightened and brightened

with value-setting Venus's creative quintile
with Uranus. You can be smart and socially
skillful at the same time.

★ **DECEMBER 14–16**
face the music
If you hit a wall of resistance from others, you
will be tempted to jump over it or ignore its
presence. Mars in extra-polite Libra aligns
with Saturn in stubborn Scorpio, presenting
a barrier that impedes your progress on
December 14. However, an escapist Mercury-
Jupiter quincunx on the **16th** prompts you to
refuse to face facts. But denial is only a delaying
tactic, so it's wiser to buckle down and address
a difficult task or unpleasant person right away.
Honestly dealing with the issues enables you
to build trust and create the time and space for
thinking about more interesting subjects.

★ **DECEMBER 25**
break from the past
A reactive Mars-Uranus opposition doesn't
advise following rules, executing plans, or
taking orders from anyone. This high-tension

alignment may elicit accidents or outbursts
of anger; however, you can overcome your
boredom with age-old traditions by simply
inventing new ones. Just don't spring them
on anyone without warning. If you tell others
that this is an experiment, the pressure
to succeed is reduced and acceptance of
alternatives can grow.

SUPER NOVA DAYS

★ **DECEMBER 29–31**
no turning back
Mercury joins the Sun on **December 29**, which
usually clarifies thinking and empowers
speech; however, their squares to erratic
Uranus on **December 29–30** can overload your
nervous system and galvanize your desire for
independence. The revolution that counts,
though, is the one within. Be certain of what
the real battle entails, because a relentless
Mars-Pluto square on the **30th** means you're
playing for keeps. Mercury's conjunction
with Pluto and square to Mars on the **31st**
underscore the importance of any changes
you make.

APPENDIXES

★

2013 MONTH-AT-A-GLANCE ASTROCALENDAR

★

FAMOUS AQUARIANS

★

AQUARIUS IN LOVE

TUESDAY 1

WEDNESDAY 2

THURSDAY 3 ★ **SUPER NOVA DAYS** Avoid responding recklessly

FRIDAY 4 ★

SATURDAY 5 ★

SUNDAY 6 ★

MONDAY 7 ★

TUESDAY 8

WEDNESDAY 9

THURSDAY 10

FRIDAY 11 ●

SATURDAY 12 ★ Explore unconventional forms of fun

SUNDAY 13

MONDAY 14

TUESDAY 15

WEDNESDAY 16

THURSDAY 17

FRIDAY 18

SATURDAY 19 ★ Temper your radical behavior with a spoonful of sweetness

SUNDAY 20 ★

MONDAY 21

TUESDAY 22

WEDNESDAY 23

THURSDAY 24 ★ Further research may be needed to build a solid case

FRIDAY 25 ★

SATURDAY 26 ○

SUNDAY 27

MONDAY 28

TUESDAY 29

WEDNESDAY 30 ★ Work responsibilities come first today

THURSDAY 31

★ designates key date

FRIDAY 1	
SATURDAY 2	
SUNDAY 3	
MONDAY 4	
TUESDAY 5	
WEDNESDAY 6 ★	**SUPER NOVA DAYS** Iron out conflicts with others

THURSDAY 7 ★	
FRIDAY 8	
SATURDAY 9 ★	Common sense comes in handy

SUNDAY 10 ★ ●	
MONDAY 11 ★	
TUESDAY 12	
WEDNESDAY 13	
THURSDAY 14	
FRIDAY 15 ★	You can operate at a very high level of efficiency now

SATURDAY 16 ★	
SUNDAY 17	
MONDAY 18	
TUESDAY 19 ★	Avoid playing games with those you love

WEDNESDAY 20 ★	
THURSDAY 21 ★	
FRIDAY 22 ★	
SATURDAY 23	
SUNDAY 24	
MONDAY 25 ○	
TUESDAY 26	
WEDNESDAY 27	
THURSDAY 28	

FRIDAY 1	
SATURDAY 2	
SUNDAY 3	
MONDAY 4 ★	An old financial scheme could reappear today
TUESDAY 5	
WEDNESDAY 6	
THURSDAY 7 ★	Narrow your focus and concentrate on one task at a time
FRIDAY 8 ★	
SATURDAY 9 ★	
SUNDAY 10	
MONDAY 11 ●	
TUESDAY 12	
WEDNESDAY 13	
THURSDAY 14	
FRIDAY 15	
SATURDAY 16	
SUNDAY 17	
MONDAY 18	
TUESDAY 19	
WEDNESDAY 20	
THURSDAY 21	
FRIDAY 22 ★	**SUPER NOVA DAY** Try your hand at new experiences
SATURDAY 23	
SUNDAY 24	
MONDAY 25	
TUESDAY 26 ★	Don't promise more than you can deliver
WEDNESDAY 27 ○	
THURSDAY 28 ★	You can find wondrous things around every corner
FRIDAY 29	
SATURDAY 30	
SUNDAY 31	

MONDAY 1 ★ Follow the courage of your convictions

TUESDAY 2

WEDNESDAY 3

THURSDAY 4

FRIDAY 5

SATURDAY 6 ★ Romantic fantasies and artistic flights of fancy tempt you

---

SUNDAY 7 ★

MONDAY 8

TUESDAY 9

WEDNESDAY 10 ●

THURSDAY 11

FRIDAY 12

SATURDAY 13

SUNDAY 14 ★ Know your limits today

MONDAY 15

TUESDAY 16

WEDNESDAY 17 ★ Make your point and move on

THURSDAY 18

FRIDAY 19

SATURDAY 20 ★ **SUPER NOVA DAYS** Patience and pragmatism are vital

---

SUNDAY 21 ★

MONDAY 22 ★

TUESDAY 23

WEDNESDAY 24

THURSDAY 25 ○

FRIDAY 26

SATURDAY 27

SUNDAY 28

MONDAY 29

TUESDAY 30

WEDNESDAY 1 ★ Clarify your priorities today

THURSDAY 2

FRIDAY 3

SATURDAY 4

SUNDAY 5 ★ Relationships are rattled now

MONDAY 6 ★

TUESDAY 7

WEDNESDAY 8

THURSDAY 9 ●

FRIDAY 10

SATURDAY 11

SUNDAY 12

MONDAY 13

TUESDAY 14

WEDNESDAY 15

THURSDAY 16 ★ Let go of the past and live more freely in the present

---

FRIDAY 17 ★

SATURDAY 18 ★

SUNDAY 19

MONDAY 20 ★ Thinking through a difficult problem pays off

TUESDAY 21

WEDNESDAY 22

THURSDAY 23

FRIDAY 24

SATURDAY 25 ○

SUNDAY 26 ★ **SUPER NOVA DAYS** Give peace a chance

MONDAY 27 ★

TUESDAY 28 ★

WEDNESDAY 29

THURSDAY 30

FRIDAY 31

SATURDAY 1 ★ Leap over resistance with a radically new perspective

SUNDAY 2

MONDAY 3

TUESDAY 4

WEDNESDAY 5

THURSDAY 6

FRIDAY 7 ★ Embrace the unknown

SATURDAY 8 ★ ●

SUNDAY 9

MONDAY 10

TUESDAY 11

WEDNESDAY 12 ★ Being flexible on the job is a smart strategy

THURSDAY 13

FRIDAY 14

SATURDAY 15

SUNDAY 16

MONDAY 17 ★ **SUPER NOVA DAYS** Your excitement is effervescent

TUESDAY 18 ★

WEDNESDAY 19 ★

THURSDAY 20

FRIDAY 21

SATURDAY 22

SUNDAY 23 ○

MONDAY 24

TUESDAY 25

WEDNESDAY 26

THURSDAY 27 ★ Expressing yourself openly is a risk worth taking

FRIDAY 28 ★

SATURDAY 29

SUNDAY 30

MONDAY 1 ★ Redefine your expectations of others

TUESDAY 2

WEDNESDAY 3

THURSDAY 4 ★ Take a different approach to a complicated relationship

---

FRIDAY 5 ★

SATURDAY 6 ★

SUNDAY 7 ★

MONDAY 8 ●

TUESDAY 9

WEDNESDAY 10

THURSDAY 11

FRIDAY 12

SATURDAY 13

SUNDAY 14

MONDAY 15

TUESDAY 16

WEDNESDAY 17 ★ Discover surprising new sources of joy

THURSDAY 18 ★

FRIDAY 19 ★

SATURDAY 20 ★

SUNDAY 21

MONDAY 22 ★ ○ **SUPER NOVA DAY** Be reasonable and responsible

---

TUESDAY 23

WEDNESDAY 24

THURSDAY 25

FRIDAY 26

SATURDAY 27

SUNDAY 28

MONDAY 29

TUESDAY 30

WEDNESDAY 31 ★ You can invent brilliant ways to manage tasks

THURSDAY 1 ★ **SUPER NOVA DAYS** Turn awkward moments into playful ones

---

FRIDAY 2 ★

SATURDAY 3 ★

SUNDAY 4 ★

MONDAY 5

TUESDAY 6 ●

WEDNESDAY 7

THURSDAY 8

FRIDAY 9

SATURDAY 10

SUNDAY 11 ★ Think clearly, speak slowly, and remain patient

MONDAY 12 ★

TUESDAY 13 ★

WEDNESDAY 14 ★

THURSDAY 15

FRIDAY 16

SATURDAY 17

SUNDAY 18

MONDAY 19 ★ Reconcile your diverse needs for stimulation and safety

---

TUESDAY 20 ★ ○

WEDNESDAY 21

THURSDAY 22 ★ Concentration is difficult; relax and remain open-minded

---

FRIDAY 23

SATURDAY 24

SUNDAY 25

MONDAY 26

TUESDAY 27 ★ Overestimating the value of others is likely now

---

WEDNESDAY 28

THURSDAY 29

FRIDAY 30

SATURDAY 31

SUNDAY 1

MONDAY 2 ★ Small differences can provoke arguments

TUESDAY 3 ★

WEDNESDAY 4 ★

THURSDAY 5 ●

FRIDAY 6

SATURDAY 7

SUNDAY 8

MONDAY 9 ★ A setback or lack of progress at work is possible

TUESDAY 10 ★

WEDNESDAY 11 ★

THURSDAY 12

FRIDAY 13

SATURDAY 14 ★ SUPER NOVA DAYS Simplify your ideas now

SUNDAY 15 ★

MONDAY 16 ★

TUESDAY 17

WEDNESDAY 18

THURSDAY 19 ★ O Stretch your mind and your awareness will grow

FRIDAY 20

SATURDAY 21

SUNDAY 22

MONDAY 23

TUESDAY 24

WEDNESDAY 25

THURSDAY 26 ★ Enjoy the company of colleagues

FRIDAY 27 ★

SATURDAY 28 ★

SUNDAY 29

MONDAY 30

TUESDAY 1 ★ **SUPER NOVA DAYS** Reassess your values and resources

---

WEDNESDAY 2 ★
THURSDAY 3 ★
FRIDAY 4 ●
SATURDAY 5
SUNDAY 6
MONDAY 7 ★ Cooperation may be hard to find now

TUESDAY 8 ★
WEDNESDAY 9
THURSDAY 10
FRIDAY 11
SATURDAY 12
SUNDAY 13
MONDAY 14
TUESDAY 15
WEDNESDAY 16 ★ Try an irreverent approach to overcome obstacles

---

THURSDAY 17
FRIDAY 18 ○
SATURDAY 19
SUNDAY 20
MONDAY 21
TUESDAY 22
WEDNESDAY 23
THURSDAY 24 ★ Forgiving, forgetting, and letting go come easily

---

FRIDAY 25 ★
SATURDAY 26
SUNDAY 27
MONDAY 28
TUESDAY 29
WEDNESDAY 30
THURSDAY 31 ★ Resolve an issue by using unconventional tactics

---

FRIDAY 1	
SATURDAY 2	
SUNDAY 3	●
MONDAY 4	
TUESDAY 5	
WEDNESDAY 6 ★	Trust your instincts

THURSDAY 7	
FRIDAY 8	
SATURDAY 9	
SUNDAY 10	
MONDAY 11	
TUESDAY 12 ★	Taking calculated risks is strategically appropriate

WEDNESDAY 13	
THURSDAY 14 ★	**SUPER NOVA DAYS** Uncover unexpressed talents

FRIDAY 15 ★	
SATURDAY 16 ★	
SUNDAY 17	○
MONDAY 18	
TUESDAY 19	
WEDNESDAY 20	
THURSDAY 21	
FRIDAY 22	
SATURDAY 23	
SUNDAY 24	
MONDAY 25 ★	Focus on the most important issue of the day

TUESDAY 26	
WEDNESDAY 27	
THURSDAY 28	
FRIDAY 29	
SATURDAY 30 ★	Collaborating with clever colleagues ignites brilliance

SUNDAY 1

MONDAY 2 ●

TUESDAY 3

WEDNESDAY 4

THURSDAY 5

FRIDAY 6 ★ Facts are fuzzy; take what you hear with a grain of salt

SATURDAY 7 ★

SUNDAY 8

MONDAY 9

TUESDAY 10 ★ Your full arsenal of intelligence and ingenuity is firing

WEDNESDAY 11

THURSDAY 12

FRIDAY 13

SATURDAY 14 ★ Denial is only a delaying tactic; face the music now

SUNDAY 15 ★

MONDAY 16 ★

TUESDAY 17 ○

WEDNESDAY 18

THURSDAY 19

FRIDAY 20

SATURDAY 21

SUNDAY 22

MONDAY 23

TUESDAY 24

WEDNESDAY 25 ★ Break from the past and invent new traditions

THURSDAY 26

FRIDAY 27

SATURDAY 28

SUNDAY 29 ★ **SUPER NOVA DAYS** The revolution that counts is within

MONDAY 30 ★

TUESDAY 31 ★

FAMOUS AQUARIANS

Edwin "Buzz" Aldrin	★	1/20/1930
Plácido Domingo	★	1/21/1941
Jack Nicklaus	★	1/21/1940
Diane Lane	★	1/22/1965
Sir Francis Bacon	★	1/22/1561
Sam Cooke	★	1/22/1935
Jeanne Moreau	★	1/23/1928
Chita Rivera	★	1/23/1933
Édouard Manet	★	1/23/1832
Neil Diamond	★	1/24/1941
Edith Wharton	★	1/24/1862
Alicia Keys	★	1/25/1981
Virginia Woolf	★	1/25/1882
Wayne Gretzky	★	1/26/1961
Angela Davis	★	1/26/1944
Paul Newman	★	1/26/1925
Eddie Van Halen	★	1/26/1955
Donna Reed	★	1/27/1921
Mikhail Baryshnikov	★	1/27/1948
Lewis Carroll	★	1/27/1832
Wolfgang Amadeus Mozart	★	1/27/1756
Susan Sontag	★	1/28/1933
Jackson Pollock	★	1/28/1912
José Martí	★	1/28/1853
Oprah Winfrey	★	1/29/1954
Tom Selleck	★	1/29/1945
Dick Cheney	★	1/30/1941
Phil Collins	★	1/30/1951
Franklin D. Roosevelt	★	1/30/1882
Carol Channing	★	1/31/1923
Jackie Robinson	★	1/31/1919
Norman Mailer	★	1/31/1923
Nolan Ryan	★	1/31/1947
Lisa Marie Presley	★	2/1/1968
Langston Hughes	★	2/1/1902
Clark Gable	★	2/1/1901
Rick James	★	2/1/1948

FAMOUS AQUARIANS

Ayn Rand	★	2/2/1905
Farrah Fawcett	★	2/2/1947
James Joyce	★	2/2/1882
Norman Rockwell	★	2/3/1894
Gertrude Stein	★	2/3/1874
Rosa Parks	★	2/4/1913
Henry "Hank" Aaron	★	2/5/1934
Zsa Zsa Gabor	★	2/6/1919
Axl Rose	★	2/6/1962
Bob Marley	★	2/6/1945
Ronald Reagan	★	2/6/1911
Garth Brooks	★	2/7/1962
Sinclair Lewis	★	2/7/1885
Chris Rock	★	2/7/1965
Charles Dickens	★	2/7/1812
James Dean	★	2/8/1931
Carmen Miranda	★	2/9/1909
Carole King	★	2/9/1942
Mia Farrow	★	2/9/1945
George Stephanopoulos	★	2/10/1961
Roberta Flack	★	2/10/1939
Jennifer Aniston	★	2/11/1969
Thomas Alva Edison	★	2/11/1847
Burt Reynolds	★	2/11/1936
Sheryl Crow	★	2/11/1962
Charles Darwin	★	2/12/1809
Abraham Lincoln	★	2/12/1809
Jerry Springer	★	2/13/1944
Gregory Hines	★	2/14/1946
Matt Groening	★	2/15/1954
Ice-T	★	2/16/1958
Paris Hilton	★	2/17/1981
Michael Jordan	★	2/17/1963
Toni Morrison	★	2/18/1931
John Travolta	★	2/18/1954
Yoko Ono	★	2/18/1933
Dr. Dre	★	2/18/1965

AQUARIUS IN LOVE

AQUARIUS & ARIES (MARCH 21–APRIL 19)

You are an original and independent person who needs to contribute to the common good. You can be fun-loving and friendly in a quirky, unemotional, intellectual way. You may enjoy group activities within a circle of friends. You have a strong mind and are often at the cutting edge of technology, spirituality, and culture. Fireworks can go off when you get together with an impulsive Aries, who may be as innovative and independent as you. Aries partners are always ready for new projects, and tend to project happy, courageous dispositions. Rams like to do things their own way, which can interfere with some social interactions. You may get frustrated, especially when your Aries lover is being headstrong or impatient. Although you two are typically compatible, this trait can make it tough for you to work together well with mutual interest. This dilemma can get in the way, especially when planning your social calendar. If you have Venus in Capricorn or Pisces, this problem can become difficult to resolve, although your Moon in a fire sign can increase compatibility. Together, you can make an exciting and active couple.

AQUARIUS & TAURUS (APRIL 20–MAY 20)

Your eclectic social views attract you to unique kinds of family arrangements. You seek to align yourself with individuals who share your passionate social values and sometimes radical ideals. You're much more interested in sustaining intellectual friendship than romantic love, although you can be extremely devoted and loving once committed. Even as a parent, you tend to be friendly and aloof, and can encourage your children to find their own lot in life. This is the opposite of the fiercely simplistic Bull, who is connected to basic values of home, security, and finances. Once your lover lets you into his or her heart and house, you may have to put up with exes, children, and extended family for a lifetime, since it's almost impossible for a Taurus to let go. This loyalty is at the core of the Taurus's foundation. You may find your mate's stubbornness and tenacity a bit smothering. If you have the Moon in an earth sign (Taurus, Virgo, or Capricorn) or water sign (Cancer, Scorpio, or Pisces), your chances of a happy relationship are dramatically improved. Once the two of you find the right niche for your friendship and love, you can endure a long life of progressive growth and deep love together.

AQUARIUS & GEMINI (MAY 21–JUNE 20)

You are drawn to intelligent individuals who are superior communicators. You may not tolerate mediocre thinkers, as you relate more to those who express progressive ideas with intellectual finesse. When you meet quick-witted and mentally agile Gemini, you can be swept off your intellectual feet, for the way to your heart is through language and ideas. You'll get along famously with your chatty Gemini friend—both of you can plunge into end-less pools of cultural, personal, and interpersonal communication. You'll look for ways to express your love for one another through eclectic ideas and carefully communicated perceptions. You make a life together that defies normal classifications. The biggest potential problem for this relationship is the lack of grounded practicality and your mutual eagerness to move away from emotions and toward rational logic. If either of you has the Moon in a water or earth sign, you'll have a better chance to stabilize your relationship for the long haul. If not, this may be a wonderful relationship that doesn't last very long. You're friendly as a couple, and your home will reflect your diverse interests as the two of you carve out a life that attracts a variety of people.

AQUARIUS & CANCER (JUNE 21–JULY 22)

You're happiest when you have enough space to be as eclectic as you need to be. Your main planet Uranus symbolizes enlightenment and freedom. You thrive on the dynamics of intellectual exchange and mutual friendship. It is true that you can be an outstanding friend, yet in relationships, you can maintain an emotional distance so as not to become immersed in the other person's feelings. On the other hand, your Cancer lover needs close emotional contact and reassurance. The Moon is Cancer's key planet; it binds them to their emotions, draws them into sensitive encounters with loved ones, and requires them to feel their changing moods—like the changing tides. Your Cancer mate can easily give emotional support to others, but finds it difficult to ask for what he or she needs. Obviously, there are some differences between the two of you and you'll each need to adjust your basic nature in order to maintain a solid, loving rapport. If Venus in your chart is in Pisces or if the Moon is in any water sign (Cancer, Scorpio, or Pisces), you'll feel more comfortable hanging out in the emotional realms with your lover. You'll need to get past your fear of emotional attachment so you can strike a balance.

AQUARIUS & LEO (JULY 23–AUGUST 22)

You enjoy the splendor of community life and all of the attention attached to it. You like to be a key cog in a greater wheel of activity that's able to produce impressive results. Otherwise, you may feel like you're lacking purpose and become intolerant of yourself and others. In many ways, Leos are your opposite. They love the fanfare of dramatic exhibition. They need the group, not to feel part of it, but to be recognized and appreciated by it. Your Leo lover needs your ongoing approval in order to continue to thrive. On the other hand, you tend to be self-motivating and may not be interested in fluffing the feathers of Leo's ego. Your lover is more vulnerable than you realize, and can be hurt by your natural aloofness. You and Leo are opposite signs on the zodiac wheel and, therefore, you can each add to the other's perspective of life. Success will depend upon your individual willingness to change, grow, and share. If the Moon or Mars in your chart is in a fire sign (Aries, Leo, or Sagittarius), your chances for compatibility are improved as you'll tend to share more activities and interests. This is a dynamic relationship that can combine your two very different individual lifestyles into an enduring partnership.

AQUARIUS & VIRGO (AUGUST 23–SEPT. 22)

You're community-oriented with a strong desire to express your intellectual interests that will, in some way, pave the way to a better future. Your Virgo lover is connected to the planet Mercury and is also intellectually astute in observing the higher needs of the world-at-large. Efficient, organized Virgos appeal to your keen mental abilities. This is a relationship that begins and stays on a mental plane. Even the physical act of making love is first and foremost a mental activity for the two of you; if you can't do it in your mind and if you can't talk about it, it may not be satisfactory. One of the issues you face is how differently you each approach life. You're driven by originality, offering new insight into all endeavors. Your Virgo is driven by precision, focusing on details rather than broad concepts. He or she will probably seem too caught up in the practical limitations of your new ideas and you may tire of the criticism, however well intended. If Mercury or Venus in your chart is in Capricorn, or with your Moon in any earth sign (Taurus, Virgo, or Capricorn) chances for compatibility are improved. This can be a rewarding relationship if you can learn to accept Virgo's need for analysis and detail.

AQUARIUS & LIBRA (SEPT. 23–OCT. 22)

You are astutely aware of the people you choose to relate with—preferring bright and eccentric folks as friends and lovers. You're not attracted to crude and thoughtless individuals, and keep a distance from situations that offend your highly tuned sensibilities. In Libra, you meet someone who is refined, creative, and dedicated to the pursuit of beauty. All this fits your ideal and it's a good place to start a relationship. Libra's key planet is Venus, and as such they're attracted to peace in relationships and are committed to finding balance in all that they do. One problem may arise from your blunt honesty. If you're asked for the truth, you'll give it, whatever the consequences. Your radical approach to honesty can be offensive to Libra, who may wish you'd think before you speak. If Venus in your chart is in Capricorn, your utilitarian values may clash with your mate. If Venus in your chart is in Pisces, the two of you may struggle to find common ground. You're both mentally motivated air signs and can have a relationship that's stimulated by the elegance of language, even when it comes to sex. In an intimate relationship, you can both delight in the magical exploration of your sexuality as a means to reach higher realms of the soul.

AQUARIUS & SCORPIO (OCT. 23–NOV. 21)

You do not like to be suppressed and often choose to operate outside of authority. On the other hand, you can create your own rigid structures, as you're highly opinionated and can be intellectually snobbish at times. This inflexibility can bother people who share some of these traits. When you hook up with a Scorpio, you meet someone who has a lesser desire to overthrow the establishment, yet is keenly aware of power struggles and authority issues. They, too, have fixed ideas about the world, and prefer to engage with people with similar beliefs. This is the strength and weakness of this relationship. If you can find a common ground, then this union is meant to thrive. If not, you may put most of your energy into disagreements. Personal issues can be just as heated. You may also feel your Scorpio lover's too emotional. Scorpio's intensity can lead to mind-bending sex, but you may not be willing to pay the price of admission. You feel more comfortable in an intellectual relationship with less emphasis on irrational feelings. If, however, the Moon or Mars in your chart is in a water sign, you'll be more eager to jump into the emotional depths. If you two truly love each other, you'll find a way to achieve balance.

AQUARIUS & SAGITTARIUS (NOV. 22–DEC. 21)

Yours is an intellectual attachment at first, and you can enjoy your friendship with a Sagittarius, remaining loyal and trustworthy through thick and thin. Since you're not emotionally charged, it's best for you to relate to others through rational thinking—and rationally, your Sagittarius lover scores enough points for you to pursue the relationship. The Archer makes a fine companion for you. He or she is goal- oriented and dynamic in their global interests. Whereas you tend to be motivated by originality, your partner is motivated by high ideals. This is a good mix, for you can easily share your vision with good humor and intelligence. Your Sagittarius lover may not be cuddly, but that's okay with you. You'll gladly allow your mate the room needed to follow his or her adventurous spirit, if in return he or she gives you the emotional distance you need to feel comfortable. If the Moon or Mars in your chart is in Virgo or Pisces, compatibility may be more difficult, for you may have conflicting needs. Ultimately, this is an exciting and active union that produces and inspires big ideas and innovative living. The two of you are highly compatible, and can go the distance with an emotionally satisfying union.

AQUARIUS & CAPRICORN (DEC. 22–JAN. 19)

You live according to a set of values that are based on humanity rather than individuality. One of your strengths is your ability to remain detached from heated debates or controversy. In fact, you may avoid confrontation, especially when emotions are flying about. Capricorns are dignified in their pursuit of accomplishment, and can appear unemotional or distant in personal situations. As you each may choose to avoid emotional realms— for different reasons—intimacy may be challenging. You may find your sure-footed Goat too conservative for your nontraditional tastes, while he or she thinks you're weird. Yet if you can learn to appreciate the stability he or she may offer, you'll actually be more able to live your life on the edge. Of course, you'll need an exceptional Capricorn—one who won't judge your tendency to throw away the past in order to embrace the future. You two can maintain a high degree of respect for one another, although you may find it difficult to express tender affection and vulnerable feelings. If your Moon is in an earth or water sign, chances for compatibility are increased. You must express your respect and love to each other, allowing trust to develop and overcome your differences.

AQUARIUS & AQUARIUS (JAN. 20–FEB. 18)

When two individuals with the same sun sign meet, there is often immediate compatibility. The big question is whether your Aquarian mirror image can bring to the relationship enough qualities that you need and do not already possess. Your Aquarian may be just as quirky as you are, but if you have each been pulled into different lifestyles, it may be impossible for you to find a compromise. You'll need to give eachother wide latitude, allowing free expression to override emotional attachment. This need for freedom can be so strong that it takes precedence over the relationship, dooming it to an early, but amicable ending. If either of you (both is better) have the Moon or Mars in an earth or water sign, chances for a long-term union are increased. Regardless of other planets, the two of you will probably be busy in friendship circles, sharing the same inspiration from political and community news. Romantically, you'll need to pay special attention to find ways to spice up your sex life— emotionally and physically—if you want to share a fulfilling life. Nevertheless, the two of you can create a totally unique relationship that defies all categorization, and one that enriches you both.

AQUARIUS & PISCES (FEB. 19–MARCH 20)

Your awareness is not an emotional understanding as much as it is a rational and intelligent observance of the world around you. Meanwhile, Pisces, the last sign of the zodiac, is a kaleidoscope of intuitive understanding and compassion. Pisces folks are aware of the troubles in the world-at-large and carry this perspective forward with sensitivity, gentle care, and empathy. But they're not as intellectually oriented as you may be. This represents a basic difference of styles. You are motivated by ideas and concepts. He or she is motivated by compassion and wordless feelings. If you can get past this difference, together you are inspired to advance the mind and heart of humanity. You'll need to learn to incorporate the imaginative and intuitive gifts of your Pisces into your sometimes detached intellectual framework. If Mercury or Venus in your chart is in Pisces, this will be much easier for you. In fact, if the Moon in your chart is in any water sign, you'll have an increased chance of making it work. Your lover will need to learn how to communicate in rational and nonemotional ways in order to help you understand his or her needs. If you two can achieve a balance, it will be a satisfying, enduring relationship.

ABOUT THE AUTHORS

RICK LEVINE When I first encountered astrology as a psychology undergraduate in the late 1960s, I became fascinated with the varieties of human experience. Even now, I love the one-on-one work of seeing clients and looking at their lives through the cosmic lens. But I also love history and utilize astrology to better understand the longer-term cycles of cultural change. My recent DVD, *Quantum Astrology*, explores some of these transpersonal interests. As a scientist, I'm always looking for patterns in order to improve my ability to predict the outcome of any experiment; as an artist, I'm entranced by the mystery of what we do not and cannot know. As an astrologer, I am privileged to live in an enchanted world that links the rational and magical, physical and spiritual—and yes—even science and art.

JEFF JAWER I'm a Taurus with a Scorpio Moon and Aries rising who lives in the Pacific Northwest with Danick, my double-Pisces musician wife, our two Leo daughters, a black Gemini cat, and a white Pisces dog. I have been a professional astrologer since 1973 when I was a student at the University of Massachusetts (Amherst). I encountered astrology as my first marriage was ending and I was searching for answers. Astrology provided them. More than thirty-five years later, it remains the creative passion of my life as I continue to counsel, write, study, and share ideas with clients and colleagues around the world.

ACKNOWLEDGMENTS

Thanks to Paul O'Brien, our agent, our friend, and the creative genius behind Tarot.com; Gail Goldberg, the editor who always makes us sound better; Marcus Leaver and Michael Fragnito at Sterling Publishing, for their tireless support for the project; Barbara Berger, our supervising editor, who has shepherded this book with Taurean persistence and Aquarian invention; Laura Jorstad, for her refinement of the text; and Sterling project editor Mary Hern, assistant editor Sasha Tropp, and designer Abrah Griggs for their invaluable help. We thank Bob Wietrak and Jules Herbert at Barnes & Noble, and all of the helping hands at Sterling. Thanks for the art and ideas from Jessica Abel and the rest of the Tarot.com team. Thanks as well to 3+Co. for the original design and to Tara Gimmer for the author photo.